CONVERSATIONS

JORGE PARDO
AND
JAN TUMLIR
CONVERSATIONS

INVENTORY PRESS

NEUGERRIEMSCHNEIDER BERLIN

INTRODUCTION

Jan Tumlir

Even though I had spoken casually with Jorge Pardo on several occasions before, our conversations began in earnest sometime in early 1999, shortly after I had written a review of his Focus show at the Museum of Contemporary Art, Los Angeles—the first iteration of his "house-that-is-also-a-sculpture" conceit, *4166 Sea View Lane*—for the now-defunct magazine *Artext*. Jorge contacted me upon reading the piece and suggested we meet for coffee to discuss some of the points I had raised. During that encounter, he communicated to me his general frustration with the critical establishment in Los Angeles, and in particular with its response to his work. Much of the press that he initially received in his hometown was negative, but this was not really the gist of his complaint. Jorge argued that his fiercest critics were baffled by his work, that they were fundamentally ill-equipped to put it into context and were therefore performing a public disservice by considering it at all. It occurred to me then that this was an artist who actually valued criticism, and moreover one who believed that art and writing could be mutually beneficial. As our conversation progressed, I got the distinct impression that I was being recruited to write about him more, and to do so, with his assistance, better. But implied in this proposal was also the notion of a more general reciprocity: that better writing could make for better art.

It is perhaps difficult to imagine today the dearth of critical writing about L.A. art in L.A., an endemic condition that persisted through the turn of this century, which is not so very long ago. When I began my career in this field in the early nineties, local artists scarcely expected to receive any critical response to their work. In fact, this state of affairs could even be understood as decisive in regard to what they produced, a causal factor in what was routinely characterized as the "renegade" aspect of the work from the region. Certainly, this is what the critic Terry R. Myers (taking a cue from the painter Lari Pittman) was getting at with his theory of "benign neglect," as developed in his essay for the catalogue that accompanied *Sunshine and Noir*, a survey of L.A. art mounted in 1997 at the Louisiana Museum in Denmark. His argument was that art in L.A. thrived like a weed due precisely to a lack of theoretical irrigation. It is also worth noting that these thoughts were aired in the context of an exhibition approaching local practices from afar, and that this was in fact one of the first attempts to offer any kind of comprehensive assessment of these practices. I quoted Myers' text in my contribution to the coffee table primer *LA Artland*, which was published, in 2005, in London. It seemed at the time that every attempt to lucidly grapple with what was happening in L.A. could only happen elsewhere. In 2006, the Centre

Pompidou in Paris, deploying the full scope of its scholarly and cura-
torial resources, launched the mega-exhibition *Los Angeles, 1955–1985:
Birth of an Art Capital*, effectively gaining the last word on the matter. It
was not until the Getty Foundation–sponsored initiative *Pacific Standard
Time: Art in L.A., 1955–1985*, which took place in multiple venues across
the Southland in the fall of 2011, that any comparable effort was tried out
on home turf.

Obviously, Jorge wanted to somehow amend this situation. He could
afford to do so; his career was on the ascent. Just a decade out of art
school (having earned a BFA from Art Center College of Design in 1988),
he already wielded a certain art world clout. We began our conversation in his house at 4166 Sea View Lane, shortly after it had ceased to
function as a public exhibition and he had moved in. This move, which
was factored into the piece from the outset, had become the talk of
the town. The MOCA Focus shows had up until then been housed in a
modest project space within the institution, but Jorge had transplanted
the venue to a lot in Mount Washington, where he went on to construct
the sculpture-house that he inhabited for the next eight years.
Predictably, this generated a very considerable outcry from those who
saw the work as essentially opportunistic and self-serving. This reading, although unfortunate, did not in itself qualify as a misjudgment,
however; certainly it is a *question* posed by the work as to whether it is
made more for the audience or the artist. Just who is it that "gets it" in
the end? Yet Jorge's problem with the response in this case was that it
just circumvented the question—which is perhaps a central question in
art—in favor of an all too easy indictment. In fact, his problem was twofold: his critics were refusing to engage with what he understood as
the actual stakes in the work, but equally vexing to him was the fact that
the unfavorable press had absolutely no impact on his success as an
artist. It could even be argued that the most antagonistic reviews actually assisted his rise, inflating the quality of transgression in the work
and thereby stimulating public curiosity, while also convincing the art
establishment of dealers, curators, and collectors that, by supporting
him, they were onto something ostensibly radical. Jorge did not want
to be slotted into a lineage of antiestablishment production, which
he understood as long past its sell-by date, a fundamentally cynical and
bankrupt position by this point in time. He did not want to be relegated
to the status of a Conceptual prankster, which is precisely what was
implied in a great deal of the locally published writing on his work.
In short, it seemed to me that his problem came down to the fact that

he was perceived as "naughty"—a favorite pejorative term of his—and did not want to succeed in this way. Naughty artists get caught in a reactionary framework as opposed to a "discursive" one—a positive term for him. If such a framework did not yet exist for his work, at least not in L.A., then we would have to produce it from scratch. At any rate, this is how I interpreted our mutual project at the time.

Shortly after the publication of my *4166 Sea View Lane* review, Jorge asked me to write an essay for the catalogue to an exhibition that was to be mounted at The Royal Festival Hall in London. This show would feature a sleek sailboat that he had purchased in Santa Cruz, California, several years earlier, and which had been previously included in his show at the Museum of Contemporary Art in Chicago, in 1997. In advance of this project, he took me on a field trip of sorts to the San Pedro harbor to witness the boat's preparation for its voyage "across the pond." The elaborate procedure of dismantling, crating, and loading the boat as cargo onto another boat, although it was carried out straight-faced and with maximal efficiency, was of course somewhat absurd—one might say, surreal. Jorge, I gathered, was here schooling me in one of the first principles of his practice: a thing is never just a thing. A thing exists within a system of things; it comprises just one part of a larger ensemble; its use value can never be reduced to whatever it is that we might want to use it for; and, moreover, its function within the economy, as a commodity, is "mysterious," as Marx long ago pointed out. Every existing thing has a complex history, a life cycle of which we glimpse only a fractional slice at any given moment that we spend with it. Yet, on occasion, such a moment can also be seized as an auspicious point of intersection between subjects and objects, one that is pregnant with potential, engendering endless opportunities for a productive confusion of terms within the equation. Which is which? Which is the actant and which is acted upon? Art can produce moments of instability in our encounters with the material world that are productive because they force us to revise our in-built assumptions—that is, the blunt directives that allow us to operate in and on the world quasi-automatically and without friction. Jorge consistently aims for such moments, which have to be understood, first of all, as aesthetic moments, or moments in which people and things are provisionally released from the means–ends rationales that normally drive their interactions. But if this artist is to be considered a formalist—and I don't think that he would oppose this designation on principle—then it would have to be without any allegiance to the ideal of autonomous form. For Jorge, aesthetic experience pointedly does not transport one elsewhere, but rather holds one in an immanent and expansive confrontation with what actually is happening right here and now. No aesthetic form can appear within his work without bearing some acute imprint of its social surround. All such "impurities" are welcomed in as a matter of course, and the sense that not only might this not undermine the aesthetic experience, but even serve to intensify it, is what the excursion to San Pedro taught me.

Certainly, this was a privileged perspective. I had been made privy to a kind of backstory that would not appear so readily to a regular viewer in the gallery. And yet, even in its somewhat cryptic presentation at Royal Festival Hall—where this vessel in fact constituted the only object on view and did so without explanation—it begged a daunting series of questions. Where did it come from? How did it get here? And finally, what was it doing in this space? Yes, the sailboat was forcefully manipulated in all sorts of ways; it was subsumed by the intentions of an artist who staged the public's encounter with it in a manner at once deterministic and laissez-faire, prompting viewers to see it first through his eyes as this—and only this—thing, and then through their own eyes as anything that they could possibly imagine it to be. However, precisely because this boat is such a specific and predetermined object, it would also have to be given its say, dictating in no uncertain terms just what could be done with it, or how far one could go with it, as an object of art. This element of material resistance—which, perhaps paradoxically, emerges from within an invitation to free-form projection on our parts—is, I think, inherent in any object one might come across in Jorge's work. Whether it is found, store-bought, outsourced, manufactured in whole or in part elsewhere, or fabricated entirely in-studio by a team of assistants, or even by Jorge himself, it always seems to want to shrug off the role to which it is normally assigned. This, at least, was his ambition for the work as he communicated it to me during our earliest conversations, and on this point, he has remained remarkably resolute over the years.

The artistic discourse with the most traction in L.A. at the time was one that sought to erase Duchamp and his Conceptual legacy from history. The guiding impulse, as it was articulated within the pages of *Art Issues*, which was arguably the most influential organ of aesthetic theory in those years, could be qualified as a *rappel à l'ordre*. It is there that Dave Hickey famously announced that the program for the future would be all about beauty, and hence diametrically opposed to the anti-aesthetic orientation of so-called idea art as it continued to circulate through the eighties and nineties. Jorge, it seemed to me, had discovered a loophole within this equation: a found object could be beautiful, and moreover it could be remade as an object of aesthetic contemplation, but without severing its ties to the realm of mundane functionality. In fact, it was precisely due to this confrontation and compromise with even the most baleful aspects of a social order that the aesthetic nature of the thing was thrown into sharp relief. This can be said of the boat as much as the house: it stands out against its background as art precisely because it also stands in with it. Such thoughts struck me then as revelatory.

• • •

It was sometime later in 1999 that I decided to start taping the words we exchanged at semi-regular intervals. The reason behind this is that I was often astounded by what Jorge said to me—not only because it was clever, but also because it was often hilarious—and found myself paraphrasing his statements to my wife and friends, as well as to students during studio visits. Simply put, I wanted to save an accurate record for myself, but I also wanted to do so for the purpose of sharing. The thought of publishing our conversations occurred later still, and this is something that we did, in fact, discuss along the way, as is reflected in the ensuing pages.

Our conversations—those that have been recorded and transcribed here—took place over a twenty-year period, but the most concentrated part of our interaction occurred between 1999 and 2003. During this time, we met on a consistent basis—typically over lunch in a Chinatown restaurant, or in Jorge's studio in the same neighborhood, or at his house in Mount Washington—to discuss what he was working on alongside a range of other subjects of then-topical interest. A subtext worth bearing in mind as one reads what follows is that of a developing understanding between two individuals, who at first come to the table with shorthand summations of their core concerns, and then allow these to cross-pollinate and gain in complexity. Yet what strikes me, upon rereading these transcripts, is how effortlessly Jorge dives right in. References are drawn from the realms of fine art as well as literature, theater, film, and everyday life with an ease that can sometimes be off-putting, demanding a constant process of perspectival recalibration on the part of any reader in pursuit of the big picture. At the same time, it quickly emerges that this, in fact, *is* the big picture—a picture that can accommodate multiple, fractured, and otherwise seemingly irreconcilable viewpoints. The talk that transpired between us over those four years constitutes a little over half of this book.

Thereafter, we saw each other only sporadically, as Jorge began to divide his time between L.A. and Mérida, Mexico, where he transplanted a large part of his studio while working on his project *Tecoh* in the Yucatán jungle. From the house-that-is-also-a-sculpture on Sea View Lane to this extensive architectural compound built on and around the ruins of an abandoned hacienda and henequen factory there is a line of development that could be termed hypertrophic. Whereas a bona fide architect might already have an infrastructure in place to manage a project of this scale, it is a logistical feat for an artist to basically assemble it from the ground up. The construction of *Tecoh* required an outlay of financial, material, technical, and professional resources that far exceeded any project that this artist had undertaken before, and the whole process lasted almost a decade. Only once it was completed, in 2012, did we resume our conversation, meeting on three occasions in a studio that he had provisionally set up in a former post office in East L.A. This was after he had already vacated his premises in Mount Washington and cast his eye toward greener pastures. I initially sought him out to ask some questions about *Tecoh* because I was writing an essay on it for *Artforum*, but our conversation quickly transitioned to a range of related matters. General questions concerning the relation of aesthetics and politics were broached, and then later resumed via a lengthy discussion of art criticism, and in particular the writings of Benjamin H. D. Buchloh and Dave Hickey. The two conversations that followed were conducted almost entirely around the brief of sorting through their polarized ideological positions, which had been highly influential while we both were in art school, and continued to impact our thoughts, positively and negatively. These conversations stand out, on the page, as among the most focused, largely because I came to them prepared with written questions and comments in hand. It may be that, at this point, I was already trying to reach some sort of conclusion in what we had originally imagined as a project without an end.

After that, we lost touch. Jorge decamped from the West Coast, moving his studio permanently to Mexico, and dividing his time between Mérida and his new home in New York. I stuck it out in L.A., sought out new artists to serve as discussion partners, and basically shelved this whole project. It was not until the summer of 2019 that, while traveling through Berlin, I met with Tim Neuger of neugerriemschneider gallery and mentioned to him the considerable collection of conversations with Jorge that I had amassed over the years. His interest in the project rekindled my own, and upon return to California, I at once set about to organize this material. In the fall of that year, I visited Jorge in Mérida, where a final round of conversations took place. This trip afforded me the opportunity to finally visit the completed *Tecoh* complex. We discussed the project on a drive to and from the site, while also touching on its relation to his most recent project, *L'Artlatan*, a hotel in Arles, France, which had opened its doors to the public some months before. The conversations included in this last section of the book are the only ones not conducted in L.A., and a certain distance from this city that we once shared—and that allowed us to draw from a common stock of reference points—is legible in them. Nevertheless, familiar themes from prior encounters are resumed now and again, probably at my urging. The book concludes somewhat self-reflexively with a conversation about our conversation.

• • •

Although I had always thought of Jorge as an L.A. artist, it is clear that his allegiance to this place was never as stubborn as mine—which, by the way, is something he had always cautioned me about. That there is no reward for those who stay put was at the crux of his argument; in order to remain relevant, you have to get out of this town. Whether or not this is true anymore is open to debate—over the last decade or so, it would seem that the L.A. art scene has attained the global profile it always strove for—but what is undeniable is that Jorge's success as an artist was always dependent on traveling. A cursory review of his CV confirms this: fresh out of school, his first few shows were held in L.A., but in galleries with considerable international outreach. From there, connections were swiftly established to New York (Friedrich Petzel Gallery), Cologne (Galerie Gisela Capitan), Berlin (neugerriemschneider), Paris (Galerie Ghislaine Hussenot), London (Haunch of Venison), and so on. That we actually spend the greatest part of this book mulling over matters of local import testifies to a certain generosity on his part, a willingness to accommodate a more limited perspective. One striking example of this is the sheer number of times L.A.'s Museum of Contemporary Art is mentioned within these pages; while this certainly was a vital art institution during the early years of our conversations, its influence beyond L.A.'s city limits is debatable. The attempt to furnish Jorge's art with an appropriate discourse is one that begins in this place and regularly returns to it, even if only as a jumping-off point to a more propitious elsewhere.

Admittedly, this is a discussion that jumps around a great deal. An erratic pattern is set forth from the start, and it only grows more pronounced as time wears on. Lines of thought trail off, are interrupted, or else veer sharply by way of analogy in pursuit of more fruitful directions, only to be resumed at a later date. Anyone hoping to derive straight information from this book is bound to experience frustration; there is no way to get through it without some degree of tolerance for ambiguity, evasion, digression, repetition, and contradiction. Whatever challenges this might pose to reading for meaning, however, it could equally be argued that, in a book of this sort, how something is said is at least as significant as what is said. Moreover, the "how" in this case—this discourse that strenuously resists holistic reduction in favor of a kind of conceptual pile-on—tallies up very closely with the "what" of the work in question.

For the most part, these conversations have been edited as non-invasively as possible. Here and there, I have trafficked with my own words to help the overall flow, but Jorge's have largely been left standing as is. Only the last conversations in Mérida have been lightly rearranged in their order; the rest unfold in strict adherence to chronology. Simply put, the text was edited to favor its temporal unfolding over its subject matter. Within a more conventional interview format, one would typically attempt to put all related thoughts in a row, so that one topic is exhausted before moving on to the next, which is not at all what happens here. Topics trail off, go into hibernation, and then resurface; and it is the rhythms of such thought processes, which comply with the changing call-and-response patterns of a dialogue sustained over a considerable duration, that I have tried to capture with a certain fidelity.

Returning to these conversations in their entirety, I find myself shuttling between several distinct but interwoven narrative strands. First, there is an explanatory strand, which one follows strictly to learn what this artist has to say about his work in an effort to gain a clearer understanding of this work. Second, there is a biographical strand, where the thoughts and opinions that he voices are instead directed toward an understanding of the person that he is in general. Third, there is the dialogical strand, and here all of the structural dynamics that regulate talk—where no point can be stated straightforwardly, but must always answer to the promptings of an interlocutor—are thrown into sharp relief. Fourth, and this one is closely related to the last, there is the documentary strand, which is at once the finest and most volatile strand of all. It is here that the text begins to function quasi-indexically, not to communicate thoughts so much as the atmosphere in which they take shape—that is, to quote Jorge, "the conditions of the day we are speaking." Trace elements of context, considered from both a micro and macro perspective, are everywhere stamped on this language. The weather, the ambiance of the restaurants we passed through, all of the other projects that were weighing on our minds while engaged in this project, what exhibitions had recently opened and what reviews had been published, the state of art discourse and cultural criticism as it enfolded us in a particular time and place—these are just a few of the conditions impacting our talk. And then there are those that are registered more subtly, if not secretly, in this talk's shifting tones—for instance, when a moment of pronounced combativeness—why?—is followed by a moment of no less pronounced acquiescence—again, why? Words and thoughts are traded between us, and sometimes they are favorably received, dutifully cited or appropriated outright, or else they are rejected and returned to sender. Subjective contours are highlighted one moment and blurred the next, and when one attends to such cues, what comes obscurely to light are the vicissitudes of an intellectual friendship.

• • •

Even the friendliest relationships between artists and writers are complicated. From a professional standpoint, our respective investments in the process of exchange differ considerably. I'll mention one last anecdote by way of summation. In the spring of 2003, Jorge was seeking to activate the bar that he had recently designed on the ground floor of his Chinatown studio with some public programming. He suggested that to kick it off we conduct our ongoing conversation before a live audience. I readily accepted this invitation, but, no doubt due to academic compulsions, felt the need to structure the situation in such a way as to make sure we touched on certain key points. I spent the days preceding the talk preparing questions and suggestions for slides that I passed on to Jorge. Checking in on the day of the event, he assured me that he would have all the images requested at the ready, and then agreed to go over the questions an hour or two before we were due to speak. This we did in great detail and with the intellectual enthusiasm that, I was convinced, would make for an engaging evening. But, when our time came, Jorge informed me that he had put all of his slides on a fast-changing loop with no pause function. There is no place for rehearsals in his world; it is just one thing after another. "What *else* do you want to talk about?" he asked me as we prepared to begin.

1

THE IN-BETWEEN

THE UNFOLDING OF THE WORK

POST-IDEALISM

CLASS CONSCIOUSNESS

SURREALISM

CONTINGENCY

Los Angeles
1999

The first conversation in this book followed a series of more informal ones. I had begun compiling a file on Jorge, and came to our meetings armed with a tape recorder. I recall marking each tape with the date of the encounter, yet neglected to include this information in the course of transcription. A whole set of tapes was lost during a move, hence the rough assignment of a good number of the conversations that follow to a period stretching from 1999 to 2002. Nevertheless, this one is the first, and it occurred sometime in late 1999, and I recall that it took place, like so many ensuing, in a restaurant not far from Jorge's Chinatown studio. What seems remarkable is how swiftly Jorge lays all his cards on the table. The entire lexicon of his signature terms is deployed in rapid-fire succession: on the plus side there is "the speculative," "contingency," "ambivalence," and on the minus side "transcendence," "transparency," "totalization." He characterizes the context within which he operates as "post-idealistic," and then straightaway begins to identify those idealistic artists whose practices he seeks, in one way or another, to counteract. This first conversation reads almost like a crash course in what might be termed "the Pardo method."

JT   Your work is often discussed as occupying a space between different disciplines, and I wonder if maybe that's a bit facile.

JP   The epitome of the privileged space for art is "the in-between"; that's where you're supposed to rewrite the genres. That privilege is precisely the problem because what it does is allow you to handicap the actual effects of the artwork, because it absolves it of any responsibility to function. On one hand, it allows for a certain projection, but on the other hand, it doesn't concretize itself in any consequential way. If you're going to be an interesting artist,

you really have to understand your relation to other sorts
of production.

JT   There is a tendency in art to value the non-functional in itself:
a thing becomes art once it has stopped functioning in the world.

JP   When that happens, the object stops being speculative. And that
is completely detrimental because, ultimately, what I make is all
about extending and intensifying the space of the speculative.

JT   Part of what we call function in design is perhaps just the outcome
of a specific set of client relations. Art ostensibly foregoes these
relations, and in this way its lack of function takes on the allure of
a kind of freedom...

JP   What happens traditionally in art with the client relation is that
it's put into this place where it becomes just a given, a passive
condition of the work, whereas in my work it's my job to re-elab-
orate it somehow so that it appears in the physiognomy of the
work. I want to make that condition explicit, and to use it for
reflexive purposes.

JT   Generally, it gets mystified to the point of disappearing.

JP   What's really problematic about that is that, in the process, you
don't have to realize your activity. In the commercial sector, the
issue of power is not central; it's not what the work is trying
to understand. Design is completely comfortable with the idea
that it's a very powerful activity that's all about manipulation,
and inducing effects that maybe aren't so good, or maybe are
great... It's a space that can handle adequately the ambivalence
between the client, the technique, the solution, the response, and
so on, to a particular subject. On the other hand, the art world
seems to be still a very contrived space. You don't talk about commerce, or if you do, you're only allowed to do it in caricature. You
distance commerce by caricaturing it.

JT   Your stance in this regard is shaped by a particular moment, but
it is also reacting against it. We could discuss your relation to
so-called appropriation art and simulationism, for instance.

JP My background is in the eighties. That's when I learned to be artistically literate, and my work could be read as a series of responses to that. It is really trying to instrumentalize that particular period. If you were a student at that time, you had a number of subjects you could approach within a general field. But what is interesting, if you are really going to play out the theoretical side of things today, is that the work can no longer be about suspending your disbelief. It has to be about the implicating conditions. If you're going to talk about commerce, you have to be simultaneously in the commercial field. And if you're going to talk about power, you have to somehow manifest your own conditions of power. It's a difficult thing, and a lot of people don't understand this about the work, but this will make it much more interesting.

JT This is the kind of content or meaning that only becomes available over time, and through a sustained engagement with whole bodies of work. This is another characteristic of so-called eighties art: that it unfolds from one piece to the next as a series of moves that can be read, almost like a narrative. Isn't this especially true in the case of your work? That individual pieces always have to be seen against the larger unfolding of the practice? And I'm also interested in how that's no longer the case with so much younger art. We're cycling back to some sort of a notion of autonomy, the individual and autonomous object.

JP I think it's in the unfolding … It's in somehow maintaining a productivity in the unfolding. Somewhere along the line, the longevity, or the notion of longevity, sort of got the content soaked out of it. But things aren't valid just because they're old; old things are interesting when they can still carry a kind of information … I'm not quite comfortable with this idea that because you're around for a long time, that you default to some sort of relevance. You know, a lot of bad art gets made for a long time—that's more the norm than the exception. But I do think it is a lifelong project for the work, or that it is a project where duration is considered.

JT Well, I thought that's very clear in your works because one can look at every single piece as having a duration, and then that extends into the work overall, which has another sort of duration. I was thinking about how, for instance, you make a piece and then display it, but what happens afterwards, after it is sold, say, that may take that piece somewhere else entirely. The piece could be used in some way, or again displayed, but now in the home of the collector.

JP   Yeah, and the framework for that phenomenon is something that I hope I can control to some extent. One of the things I've always thought about is: why do works end up in galleries? What does that mean? It doesn't seem to make any sense ... The idea of a "shop" is completely uninteresting to me, and then the idea of a controlled area—you know, like a scientific space of speculation, the white cube, or whatever you want to call it—that's even more uninteresting.

JT   But that's precisely where "the speculative," as you put it, has traditionally taken place.

JP   Absolutely!

JT   So, when you're talking about your attempts to extend the speculative potential of works, you're really talking about extending it beyond the space of the gallery ...

JP   ... Beyond its architectural constituency. You know, we live in a kind of post-idealistic situation, and if that's the case, then you should be able to impact the context of the work instead of overriding it. It seems like the whole gallery phenomenon is defensive. It seems to be still somewhat in dialogue with those eighteenth- or nineteenth-century transcendentalists like Caspar David Friedrich, and this old idea that nature is unbearable because you can't control the way people see it. This was a time when young kids went around collecting ruins. The gallery is totally connected to that kind of history.

JT   It's totally connected to the notion that for art to have value or worth ...

JP   ... It has to be mitigated somehow. The context became incredibly vulnerable.

JT   When you read Kant or Schiller, it's almost like the passage of the object through art, through the studio and gallery, becomes this cleansing process, because the life context seemed to them so corrupt. That's why it has to be so forcefully removed in order to have this spiritual value, or whatever ...

JP   That's exactly what I'm trying to talk about. I think that we live in this post-idealistic world where you can no longer believe that it, anything, doesn't work. We live in a world where it has become so difficult, where it has become such a precise practice, to mount an interesting gallery show. It's very strange. That former notion of inside and outside is completely reformulating itself. It happens in a very blunt way: you go to a gallery, and then you go outside, and you realize that the garbage you're looking at on the ground is more interesting. Or the car you're getting into ... One of the reasons I became interested in the functional was precisely because of that problematic. The functional allows you to look at things in this other space without that kind of cleansing you're talking about. As a reflexive model, it's very useful to me.

JT   The gallery is just one station, right?

JP   Yeah. To be able to look at a position like that, you have to separate it from the kind of idealism I'm talking about.

JT   It's not exactly an avant-garde position in the sense that there is no attempt to actually negate or transcend the gallery system, the so-called institution of art. It is more nuanced, more willing to compromise. More artists seem to be thinking that way—Andrea Zittel, for instance. How do you see her operating?

JP   I think her position is very traditional. She's basically making Romantic landscape paintings. She's taking the perverse and the eccentric and the excessive in the Bauhaus and early modernist design, and treating it like a field or something—that's about how she treats it. There is this kind of distancing that happens there that's not very useful for me.

JT   Like a parody or something?

JP   Like a parody! She's like Spielberg: it's the proximity to reality that someone like Spielberg proposes in a film like *Saving Private Ryan* where it's supposed to "feel real."[1] What the fuck does that mean? It's supposed to feel like you are there in World War II. But nobody knows what that was like, not even the people who were actually there—they don't remember. It's insane! It's a big sham!

JT   I always find in your work an insistence on a kind of banality.

JP   There's always a kind of clearing out of the playing field. Take *4166 Sea View Lane* (fig. 1), for instance: it becomes an exhibition, but I live there, it's my house, it's in a regular neighborhood.[2] It's asking you to sift through all this shit, to really get involved in this stuff, and it's not making it easy. It's maintaining what's at stake in this really kind of vulnerable place.

JT   Well, there's this insistence on a kind of everyday-ness ... You propose yourself, your own life, as the literal content of that work, but you do so in a very mundane sort of way. What you're proposing is not so extraordinary or bizarre; it doesn't really conform to most expectations of the crazy artist's life.

JP   I'm not going to familiarize anyone with my life. I'm talking about the de-familiarization of everything around us, but always through a kind of sober banality. It would be interesting to see what is the potential of something that isn't trying so hard to be spectacle. How does spectacle happen, on a very base level? The work often starts with a kind of difficult leap in language, in terminologies and historical categories. As art, it is concerned with what's directly in

1   Steven Spielberg's World War II epic *Saving Private Ryan* was released in 1998, which is probably why it is coming up as a reference here. It received a great deal of attention at the time for achieving a new standard of immersive verisimilitude, especially in its almost thirty-minute opening segment, which is set on so-called Omaha Beach in German–occupied Normandy during invasion by the allied powers.

2   *Jorge Pardo, 4166 Sea View Lane* was presented as part of the MOCA Focus series at the Museum of Contemporary Art in Los Angeles. Pardo was invited by curator Ann Goldstein to participate in the series, which typically had been confined to a modest gallery within the museum. In 1993, he submitted a proposal to mount his exhibition off-site on a 9,000-square-foot lot in the Mount Washington neighborhood of L.A. There, he went on to build his "house-that-is-also-a-sculpture," a conceit that would be resumed in numerous other locations thereafter. This work was on public view from October 11 to November 15, 1998. Afterward, the artist moved into the house and lived there until 2007.

front of you, but at the same time, it wants to do something with the material that you have in your head once you leave the gallery. It refuses to acknowledge this threshold. You know, it's like, this is interesting here, but it's got to be interesting other places too, or else it's not going to work.

JT   **I would maybe say that it operates somewhere between a critical practice and a formally progressive one. You've used the words "sinister" and "poetic" to talk about this, and these two words seem to encompass that possibility of being critical and progressive at the same time. You're critiquing the givens while also proposing some new variables...**

JP   It's sort of a way to skirt around the problem of irony. It's really unproductive to develop an ironic relationship to things you're interested in. It makes much more sense to try to extract something pleasurable from them, from a contradiction, or an absurdity, or a misperception, or from something horrible... When I was in school in the eighties, it was just assumed that being poor was horrible, and that people in the Third World were lesser people because they were impoverished, and that doesn't seem to be really the case anymore. You have countries like Mexico that are incredibly wealthy, but they have a really fucked-up relation to development. I find that looking at these kinds of contradictions is really useful for structuring a work of art. That model is very effective for dealing with a kind of ambivalence toward the sorts of problems I'm talking about. It actually digests and transforms and thoroughly deals with ambivalence. Somehow, it all seems to work and, at the same time, resist a kind of moralizing. It keeps the more conservative parts of Marxism at bay.

JT   **You're talking about trying to work with these contradictions as a kind of process, but how do you frame the argument for a viewer? Often it seems that your works include impoverished materials and techniques alongside much more high-end, even state-of-the-art, ones.**

JP   What do you mean?

JT   **Like, you mentioned having some of your recent glass lamps** (fig. 2) **fired in Mexico, in these workshop conditions that were sort of below par. I think that you were contrasting the rough nature of that** process to the electrical fittings, which are produced in New York and are ultra-fine, for instance.

JP   OK, I see. In that case it worked out really nicely. I like working in Mexico because all this stuff happens there that doesn't happen in the States. There's a whole town of boys who only know how to blow glass because there is nothing else happening there. In a way, it is like this vintage postwar experience, as sick as that sounds. But there's something interesting about being able to refer to that and say, "Well, wait a minute, the world actually is different, and what's valid to these people is set on completely different terms," and I'm interested in having access to things like that in one way or another … so, it's not just about going down to Mexico. And it's not really about setting up a contradiction in terms of impoverishment and wealth. What I'm working with is a much more egalitarian type of aspiration, but, again, I really don't want to totalize it in this way.

JT   Yeah, because that way of working with pure contradiction is very familiar from Surrealism, say. The Surrealists were interested in older modes of production, or in artifacts from an earlier time, or even in the possibility of having a more archaic culture existing at the heart of this newer one. But they really saw in that older thing or culture a kind of transcendent potential.

JP   I'm not really someone who has any belief in transcendence at all as something productive. In fact, if anything, I want to make works where, in order for them to run, you have to perform the opposite operation: they become weirder as your ability to reflect on them becomes more precise. Then the contradictions begin to do things that are not about reinforcing themselves. Then you realize what it might mean for this person to make a house, and what it might mean for this house to be in this neighborhood, to be in this museum, to be up on a hill, and so on. I want the specific details of the speculations that somebody would bring to the project to work like a motor that runs the object, but without ever completely subsuming it.

JT   Your work implies to me all these different levels of access. Because, clearly, there are those people who have been primed to read your social cues, all your intricate codes of social status and class, and then there are those who haven't. And whether you can or can't, that depends entirely on your own social position, doesn't it? There are these different levels of access that are socially determined...

JP Most things in life are generally transparent to people. You don't necessarily look at this cup [holds up a coffee cup] and reduce it down to the first artifacts ever made. And what I'm trying to do with my work is not just to take you there, straight back to some origin, because there is something intrinsically interesting in being able to extend and control an operation like that, and using it to look at a range of other things. It's close to Surrealism, but it operates on a fundamentally different level: it refuses to escape into the world of fantasy. It's not about the invention of this other space. It has no allegiance to this idea of the subconscious as a whole separate world.

JT Still, I could cite, for instance, the [Georges] Bataille school of Surrealism where everything gets reduced down to an archaic kind of economics. That's a little more Marx than Freud, and maybe also a little bit closer to what you're up to?

JP The work is very dependent on currency, on emotional currency. It's not trying to make something out of nothing.

JT So many of the words that you use to describe your work have an economic ring. You talk about "currency" and "value," like when you say, "What's the value of art today?" You talk about "specula-tion," "the speculative" in regard to the meaning and value of art, but this could also allude to the stock market practice, for instance. Everywhere I see you thinking about things in economic terms...

JP I don't think that the work can happen without a relationship to class consciousness.

JT I was trying to get at this point: how different sorts of class con-sciousness imply different levels of reading or access to the work.

JP Well, it's clear that Surrealism has to use the object of an economy. It can't deform rocks lying in a field; it has to deform things that have value. And I don't know how I feel about that. My interest in these distinctions has always been via a process of assimilation. It's like when I went to college for the first time, not really knowing how someone becomes a serious student, because it wasn't really something I'd grown up with. You hear all these things about the value of education, but you really don't know...

JT   Are you saying that your relation to all of this—and to economics— is that of an outsider?

JP   I come from a culture where, like, it's a big leap to go from being a factory worker to reading critical theory. There are conse- quences to the assimilation into that culture from the other side. One of the consequences is that you have to read the world a certain way, and really accept how absurd its various conventions are, but at the same time you're attracted to the poetic spin- off of that phenomenon also. Some very strange structures get left behind.

JT   I wanted to come back to that question about the unfolding of the work. It seems to me that, not so long ago, artists had almost come to expect this sort of long-term engagement on the part of their audiences. The audience was expected to follow the evo- lution of the work from one piece, one show, to the next, and to connect the dots in a way that added up to a complete narrative, in a sense. This could be termed a syntactical mode of reception, and it is, I think, falling back out of style.

JP   Yeah, that is an eighties model of working; that was completely tied into that era's strategy for success.

JT   But that's still how I always think about work, as developing over time. I can't imagine just dealing with what is right there in front of me any longer. The individual artwork pulled out of any sort of longer-term context is a relatively mute thing to me.

JP   Right, it's like, once you've closed that door, you've shut out the historical.

JT   So much art writing today has done just that—especially in L.A. It's almost like we're back to Michael Fried and this modernist expectation that works should yield up their entire essence in a

Fig. 1 *4166 Sea View Lane*, 1998, Mount Washington, Los Angeles.

Fig. 2 Jorge Pardo, *Untitled*, 1999. Installation view, China Art Objects.

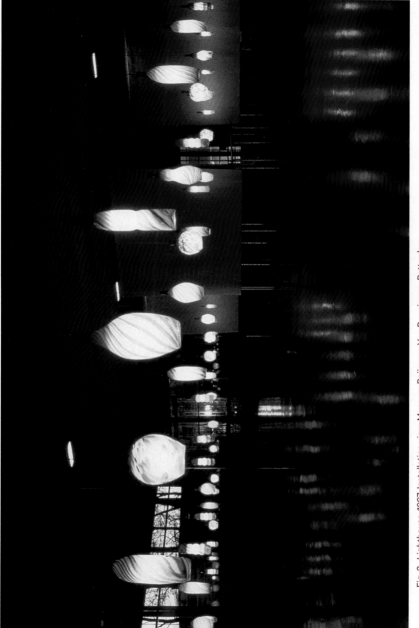

Fig. 3 *Lighthouse*, 1997. Installation view, Museum Boijmans Van Beuningen, Rotterdam.

Fig. 4 *Untitled*, 1999. Installation view, Fabric Workshop and Museum, Philadelphia.

single instant.[3] This also implies that a work should not have all that much to communicate, by the way.

JP   The idea of contingency doesn't really occur to these writers. In fact, they are trying to eliminate contingency.

JT   **You bring in contingencies, or highlight the contingencies that are already there, in order to direct the reading of your work elsewhere. You want to make your audience think backward and forward in time.**

JP   It's primarily to set up this critical analysis within the experience. There is never an autonomous moment in the work. Interesting works make data, or they just play. When you take something, some notion, and then you digress—when you start to include contingencies as a structural element, a part, of the work—it is to propose the idea that there can never be direct access. The primary impetus is speculative and analytical, but it occurs totally outside this field of religious totalization, which is what so many of your critics are aiming for. They're trying to separate the art experience from everything else in their lives; that's the only way they can evaluate a work. And I'm interested in the opposite move: I want the work to animate parts of my life that aren't really doing a whole lot … I don't think any less of a work of art because it maintains a parasitic relationship to something outside itself, or because it has dependencies. I just think that's the way it has always been. But then the further away you get from something, the more iconic it becomes, almost to the point where the really historical works of art are like complete relics.

JT   **Relics get caught up in the auratic operation …**

JP   … "It's alive, the work is alive!" It's got to output some demonstration of that—that it's an *entity*. I think it's important to resist this idea of the relic.

3   In Michael Fried's seminal essay from 1967, "Art and Objecthood," an argument is mounted against Minimalism on the basis of its temporality, the perception that it "*persists in time*" and therefore is "endless." The modernist works that the author champions are instead experienced as though they had "no duration … because *at every moment the work itself is wholly manifest*." (Fried's italics.) Michael Fried, "Art and Objecthood," in *Art and Objecthood: Essays and Reviews* (Chicago and London: University of Chicago Press, 1998), 166–67.

JT And you resist it by leaving gaps and spaces where the immediate experience of art becomes incomplete to some extent?

JP Yeah, or else it just doesn't privilege that kind of immediacy within the work. What you are asked to take on is much more insurmountable than anything a relic might allow for. And it's not as though any object could be turned into a relic, because my work is specifically set up not to do that. If you reliquate the conditions of my work, well then nothing happens... With someone like Jason Rhoades, on the other hand, it's all about the relic; it's all about privileging that sort of experience.

JT A relic is something that has been pulled out of its space-time continuum, its so-called life context. It has been isolated and categorized and basically shelved away. Its purpose and meaning are, in that sense, already accounted for. Again, it seems to me that, to avoid this condition, a work needs to remain somehow unfinished. And this is maybe ironic because Jason Rhoades' work *looks* unfinished, but really, it's not, right?

JP You have to look at work in terms of its contingencies: this part is one contingency, this part is another contingency.

JT You break your work up into different parts, or passages, always inserting a substantial gap between them. Like with the lamps, for instance: one part is made in New York, while another is made in Mexico. One contingency of the lamps, then, will reside in a certain small town in Mexico, in what can be produced there...

JP ...What can I have made there? What's the quality of those objects? What can I use that for, or what can I do with it? What can I expect the viewer to make of it? What part of the experience is going to be pleasurable or non-pleasurable? You know, is a shoddy lamp low-class? How do you make people actually look at things that don't look so good? Let me tell you something about those lamps: at first, I went to Mexico because I'd seen a lamp there that I thought I might want to have reproduced. So I went down there with my crew and made a model of the thing we were asking for, and it quickly became obvious that it wasn't going to work out, that they weren't going to remake it with any sort of accuracy. But I didn't really care, because I just wanted to see what would happen. And it was so interesting because everyone I'd come down there with had become so attached to that model in such a heavy-handed way that the only way they could see the discrepancies were as failures. I mean, these new lamps had come out really crude, and they didn't resemble the model at all, but so what? This was for a show in Rotterdam (*Lighthouse*, 1997, Museum Boijmans Van Beuningen, Rotterdam, Holland) (fig. 3), where nobody had any kind of relation to the model at all, and it was totally irrelevant whether, or to what extent, these new lamps conformed or diverged from it. But what was so interesting is that my crew couldn't see it at all: that these things were actually really beautiful—or, at least, they were to the people who made them and who were charmed by them. And what I like to do is to capitalize on these sorts of shifts, because the object should not be beholden to this kind of tyranny of the idea.

JT **But so much art gets made that way: you get an idea, you execute it.**

JP It's almost sadomasochistic. A better way to work is to leave your-self open, and actually see what happens to those things you're supposed to be in control of. Even in the things you're most in control of there has to be some doubt.

2

REPRODUCTION
ART AND ARCHITECTURE
THE READYMADE VERSUS THE RELATIONAL OBJECT
CONTINGENCY AND CONTAMINATION
DISAPPOINTMENT

Los Angeles
c. 1999–2002

Following the opening of his first house-that-is-also-a-sculpture, *4166 Sea View Lane*, Jorge began to be known as a "project artist"; increasingly, he was invited to effect interventions within existing architectural structures or design wholly new ones. This conversation begins with a brief mention of the catalogue he was working on to accompany his recently completed redesign of the lobby of The Fabric Workshop in Philadelphia. Shortly thereafter, the relations of art and architecture are considered more broadly, this being a theme that could be said to underwrite our talk right up until the end. Characteristically, however, it is replete with digressions, or at least what seem like digressions until they return to the subject at hand, and are instead revealed as analogies. Remarkable in this regard is a passage where Jorge manages to describe the various problems at stake in *4166 Sea View Lane* through the lens of Manet's painting. This is not to imply that he is as "great" as Manet, or that his work essentially comes out of a pictorial tradition, or conversely that the distinctions between different media—architecture, sculpture, painting—do not matter to him. Rather, what I take from this striking conflation, which in no way amounts to an afterthought, is that the extraction of certain affective qualities from one medium and their transposition into another is a crucial part of this artist's modus: to what is typically demanded of any medium, Jorge supplies something else. Manet, who will be returned to in later conversations, is here introduced as a kind of touchstone for his ability to productively disappoint his audience's expectations.

JP   I recently got a message from the Fabric Workshop—I'm right in the middle of mounting an exhibition there—and I found out that they wanted to wait until the show was up so they could get some images of the installation into the catalogue (fig. 4).[4] And so I called them up and said that I didn't want to do that. And they said, "Why? You know, we spent X amount of money on your exhibition, and now we want to have a document of it." So I said, "But you will have a document of it, just not that sort of document." Because I think that any catalogue with any picture of the show in it will force the viewer to project onto that space that it's talking about. I think there's much more interesting ways to use the catalogue … as a book, for instance, without some stupid picture of the show that's pretending it's valuable somehow for somebody who wasn't there to see what they missed. As a book, the catalogue can extend the problematic of the work on its own terms. The catalogue is completely dependent on the show, but at some point, it has to break away and do its own thing.

JT   The catalogue takes some things about the workings of photography for granted, and it seems like you want to be much more conscious in your use of the medium—that is, if you do use it.

JP   If what you expect is a picture of an artwork in a gallery and instead you get a color swatch or something, that forces you to reconsider your expectations, and why you're maybe satisfied or dissatisfied.[5] Those kinds of moves are much more interesting because they emphasize the problem of how does one articulate the incommensurable, which is ultimately what this is all about.

JT   Right. Well, that's why I got interested in what you were saying a while back about an early work of yours that now mainly exists as a slide. It lives on as this photo document. You mentioned how,

    4   Pardo was invited to participate in the artist-in-residence program at
        the Fabric Workshop and Museum in Philadelphia, in 1998. The result of
        his residency, a redesign of the institution's entryway and public reception
        areas, was opened to the public in 1999. The catalogue was published
        in 2000.

    5   The catalogue, which was designed by Pae White, does, in fact, feature
        color swatches. These adorn the edges of every page and also sit atop the
        commissioned texts. One reproduction of the show in question has been
        included, but it appears somewhat randomly within a non-chronological
        sequence of other works by the artist. The book's endpapers are modeled
        on a Chinese restaurant menu. See: *Jorge Pardo & the Fabric Workshop
        and Museum* (Philadelphia: Fabric Workshop and Museum, 2000).

in the context of a slide lecture, this work gains a special status, distinct from other slides. In a way, it's reformulated as a work in its own right, an original, but with a kind of virtual half-life.

JP   It's a work (*Untitled [Counter, Bank of America, Altadena, California]*, 1990) (fig. 5) that is much more interesting in a slide lecture than it ever was in an exhibition space. It also gives you something *real* to present. And the effect of a work like that will start trickling down, and it will begin to infect the projector, the light, how the artist is talking and why—all these things happen very differently in relation to a work like that.

JT   The work started out as what?

JP   So, I went to my local Bank of America to measure the counters, you know, in front of the bank tellers. And from these measurements, I made a series of wall-hanging sculptural works in three sizes: full size, half size, quarter size. But then I only photographed one of them, and you don't know which one.

JT   Because photographs, unlike sculptures, don't really have scale.

JP   Exactly, so this winds up being a sculptural problem.

JT   I suppose that you could present this very straightforwardly: all the steps the work has to undergo in order to wind up here and now as ... whatever it is. That whole process seems to me like a model for defining a different sort of value for the art object.

JP   It really capitalizes on the potential of a piece when its meaning starts to unravel. It wants to make that process visible.

JT   But isn't it also about extending the possibilities of meaning, or the way something becomes meaningful? Again, it seems that photography allows for a very substantial reframing of the original problems of that work, which had to do with sculpture and scale. You always seem to look at one medium through another to extend its potential. This reminds me of that recent review of your house-that-is-also-a-sculpture in *Art Issues*, the one where the writer basically started by claiming that the attempt to blur the borders between disciplines—in this case, art and design—had become irrelevant because it had been done before.[6] How can you write something like that? What, because some Russians had done it in the 'teens and twenties, that makes it irrelevant now, almost a century later, in L.A.? Doing it here and now is obviously a very different proposition, and not in spite of, but precisely because of the fact that it was done already back then. And that's not even taking into account that you're going about it with a whole different set of ambitions, critical priorities, contingencies, whatever. In a way, you're acknowledging that the object, the work, exists in time, and you can only do that through a process of repetition. That's in the nature of repeating, isn't it: to show how things change over time?

JP Obviously. I mean, just on the level of logic and argument, that writer is totally wrong. Because, you're right, this problematic position can only assert itself within a framework of repetition. The sort of problematic I'm after is completely dependent on relationships—on a relationship to duration, say—but this guy was really just interested in the bottom line, and in the notion that artists should be artists and designers should be designers, and anything else is corrupt. But, in the end, I don't give a shit about architecture, especially not the sort he's trying to protect. I have no real relation to it. An architect is not interested in designing a building that might not work; they just can't extract any kind of value from that. And, also, an architect has only the most literal sort of relationship to the idea of a model. Sure, there was this trend in the eighties where you had a whole school of architects who didn't build, you know, but even there, it's a very simplistic relation.

6   The review in question is by the architecture critic for the *Los Angeles Times* at the time, Nicolai Ouroussoff, and published in the pages of *Art Issues* magazine. Straightaway in the opening paragraph, it is made clear that what is at stake here is a sense of disciplinary propriety: "There's something unsettling for an architect when outsiders try their hand at design. It feeds the notion that what architects do is somehow elusive or ill-defined, a matter of choosing the right coffee-table reference book. So when Jorge Pardo recently completed his house and called it 'art,' one is initially tempted to regard the whole project as a pretentious sham. What, after all, does an artist know about fusing elements of scale, material, structure, and context into a cohesive structure—a task that an architect spends a lifetime investigating?" The work is declared a "sham" on both a functional and a formal level. "The irony," Ouroussoff continues, "is that Pardo's house fails exactly in those details that might have transformed his common building into an aesthetically remarkable structure." And whatever questions the work raises in crossing the lines between art and design are deemed by the critic to have been historically resolved. "The problem with such attempts to blur the boundaries between art and architecture is that these lines long ago faded into irrelevancy." Nicolai Ouroussoff, "Jorge Pardo," *Art Issues* 57 (March/April 1997): 41.

JT Well, generally, in art, it seems that the more simple or straightforward your model is, the more you can insist on the art context to fill it out discursively. Generally, also, the model has to be generic; it has to have a relatively transparent relation to real architecture in that sense—to other houses already built, let's say. But your house is not at all generic.

JP Yeah, and it's absolutely unequivocal on that point. When somebody comes to my house—I don't care who they are—they will look at it because it's not like other houses. Whether it's architecture or not is not important; it's the fact that this kind of looking happens that's the critical point.

JT I'm curious how you see that happening, exactly, that experience of reception.

JP Well, let's say, if the house had been like the one next door, or like the one across the street, none of this would happen. I'm using the house to think through all these problems about perception or reception. Like, what happens when you take all the windows out of a house? How do you frame a courtyard, in California? If you're living on a hillside, how then do you treat the view as something other than a primary condition of your design?

JT There's a whole range of questions that you're setting up and then responding to—established questions as well as created ones...

JP ...Like, that house is designed completely in relation to that neighborhood, but then it's not like any of the other houses there, and it's very conscious of how it's not like them. It's not responding so much to problems of architecture as to every other house I've seen. My primary reason for working that way has something to do with the problem of Surrealism, which just basically takes the readymade and then runs with it, and I don't think that's the most productive way to refer to things within a work of art. I'm much more interested in the possibility of generating an experience alongside something that is given.

JT You're talking about maybe customizing the readymade in some way, rather than just "assisting" it, let's say, in the Duchampian sense?

JP Yeah. You make something and it's not quite like what it's modeled on, but it's that too. And it extends the problem of the original thing a little bit further, because I think that a work can't really be taken seriously unless it creates a *real* problem. Now, the specific problems of my house emanate from its design: everything comes from the way that the thing looks. But then this also touches on its relation to the other houses around it, or its relation to MOCA, its relation to my other work, to other peoples' work … And the experience can only happen if you are in fact considering all those relationships at the same time, through a kind of simultaneity.

JT Do you see it as having a problematic relationship to all of those things you've just cited?

JP I think it has a problematic relationship, and I think it has a dependent relationship, a parasitic relationship, an ambivalent relationship … I mean, the structure of the work is pretty schizoid! It doesn't know where to stop! But that is also when the motor starts to rev and you realize that, ultimately, you're in control of this stuff. You can make all this happen. So, it's also about putting the viewer or reader of the work into this privileged position.

JT But what is, in a way, different about the house is the fact that you, the artist, are the one who's using it, even if you're also using it for the benefit of the viewer, to an extent. There's a kind of deflection occurring there, whereas other works propose that they might be used much more directly or literally by the viewer.

JP But if you start to relate these different works—like the house to the Münster pier (*Pier*, 1997) (fig. 6) and all those other works that are in galleries and that people could take to their homes and use—each one of them is made in relation to the others.[7] At a critical point, this whole system of relationships starts to turn, and the viewer, the collector, the artist, all of them start to switch places. The work becomes a machine …

JT … Or a game: it's like musical chairs or something. But, still, there are very substantial differences between the experience of a regular gallery-goer, let's say, and a collector—someone who not only looks at one of your chairs or shelving units, but considers the possibility of actual use, or again, not. This is a very different sort of take. I mean, the relational aspect of your work will tend to vary greatly from the one to the other.

JP   But I'm interested in making a work that actually manifests that problematic, as opposed to just quoting the problem, let's say ...

JT   **Maybe you're more interested in this as a problem that one needs to think about, rather than solve in some way.**

JP   Yeah, it's more interesting for me to think about what a collector might or might not be doing than to have to stop thinking about that. You know, it's much more interesting to leave this in the realm of contingencies. Because, ultimately, a gallery is just a place where the work takes off; it's not the primary site of the work and it never will be. But at the same time, I am very dependent on it. I couldn't do what I do without the existence of those kinds of conditions. It's almost a tool in that sense.

JT   **I suppose you could say that the gallery is functioning a little bit like a showroom or a store—especially since these kinds of spaces seem to resemble galleries more and more. Stores are taking a cue from art's minimal conditions of display. But, at the same time, the gallery remains fundamentally different, right?**

JP   It has to. It has to always retain a measure of ambivalence, and that's what separates it from the showroom. Ultimately, its point of purchase is different, you know? A showroom, for one thing, is not a space where you give out invitations and serve drinks to make people come, but then not ask them to buy something (*laughs*).

JT   **Well put.**

JP   But I want to call the bluff on this idea that works of art can create a space where nothing else, nothing other than art, can happen. I've always had a problem with that. Interesting works are interesting

7   Pardo's *Pier* was included in the third installment of Skuptur Projekte Münster in 1997. Originally constructed from California redwood, this structure is sited in the city's municipal park, and stretches from its shore, at approximately 157 feet in length, into Lake Aa. Whereas most contributions to Skulptur Projekte Münster are dismantled at the end of the exhibition, this work has become a permanent fixture in the city.

because of the way they lend themselves to the conditional, to the relational, to all the contingencies that surround them. They have to be made with all those things in mind.

JT **Let me get this straight: the contingencies that you're always talking about are seemingly a kind of extraneous content, or a condition that comes from outside the work—that is, outside your specific intent for the work.**

JP Contingency locates the referent of the work, but it's not the referent you're pulling in intentionally. It's because of the contingencies that your perception of the work, and your perception of me, is inevitably going to be contaminated. But interesting work stays interesting in spite of that. That's how Manet's work, for instance, could be interesting to people in the nineteenth century, in the twentieth century, and now again in the twenty-first century. It's because he has dealt with that problem of contingency.

JT **What do you mean by "contaminated?"**

JP If you set up, within your practice, a kind of openness to contingency, this can become a central means of accessing, or reading, the work.

JT **You make this happen…**

JP … You don't make this happen; you allow it to happen. One of Manet's contingencies was, let's say, his relationship to Realism, to other Realists. I don't know how much he really thought about that, but it doesn't matter. What matters is this picture that is able to forecast itself blindly into the future.

JT **I'm with Bataille on Manet: he claims that Manet's practice is all about disappointment, a strategic deflation of audience expectations. So, despite the fact that he's trading in this highly charged, controversial content, the way he actually renders or represents it is willfully muted. *Olympia* is his case in point: the treatment of her naked body is frustratingly distanced and, from this perspective, unexciting.[8]**

JP So, in some way it's related to what I'm talking about … Realism sets up an expectation that Manet's work fucks with.

JT Right, and in a way it's frustrating. And this makes me think about some of the negative critical responses your work has garnered, and how these might actually point to your success.

JP Usually it does. I mean, it depends on where it's coming from because, generally speaking, the more conservative you are, the more negatively you will tend to respond to my work, the less it will accommodate you. That's where the contingencies start to operate socially.

JT The use of the term "disappointment" in Bataille refers, I think, to the way in which Manet brings banality into his content or subject matter, which is often quite elevated. I suppose you could say that it has a contaminating effect.

JP Well, in a way it's almost pornographic. I mean, clearly, you had banality before that, with all those French writers and artists dealing with everyday life in a way that was very direct, let's say … again, we're talking about Realism …

JT But the difference here is that, first, you set up a sense of expectation for something, and then, you renege on it.

JP Well, it's like saying, "This picture is about this whore in relation to this brushstroke." You know, it's not about politicizing a gesture so much as simply opening up the possibility of talking about something like that for the very first time. That's what's interesting about the work, and also what marks its difference from someone like Courbet, for instance. Because, as direct as Courbet's work was, there's always this mitigating social science that's being proposed there. With Manet, that sense of responsibility just disappears. There, it's just about wanting to paint something weird, or wanting

8   On Édouard Manet's painting *Olympia* (1863), Bataille writes, "Her real nudity (not merely that of her body) is the silence that emanates from her, like that from a sunken ship. All we have is the 'sacred horror' of her presence—presence whose sheer simplicity is tantamount to absence. Her harsh realism—which, for the Salon public, was no more than gorilla-like ugliness—is inseparable from the concern Manet had to reduce *what he saw* to the mute and utter simplicity of *what was there*. Zola's realism *located* what is described; Manet departed from realism by virtue of the power he had—at least in Olympia—of not locating his subject *any-where* …" Georges Bataille, *Manet: The Taste of Our Time*, trans. Austryn Wainhouse and James Emmons (Paris: Skira, 1955), 67.

to put together things that don't go together, and for no other reason than just to see what might happen.

JT He's a good model to use…

JP …And that's why I use the term "contaminated": because I think it's important that the viewer never return to the artist for what is actually significant in the work. I mean, that's not a very productive way to read anything.

JT Talking about disappointment, it's revealing how you set up expectations so emphatically with your house-that-is-also-a-sculpture. Again, this is a work that actually includes you, the artist, as its central core of meaning, almost in that hermeneutic sense. But then, you're really not saying all that much there.

JP Me being at the center of it is totally irrelevant, in a sense, to gaining any sort of a handle on the context, on the meaning of that work. But that is the principal condition of that piece: that I am at the center of it and yet I don't really matter. That's what's emphatic about it. I think that the most an artist can set themselves up to be within a work is an interesting viewer of that work. You're always a viewer of what you do; you're never just a producer. Artists aren't really producers…

JT …And artworks aren't really consumed. But you can only introduce that idea by making an artwork that actually comes close to being consumed, or where there is a potential for consumption…

JP …It's about a radical similarity, because, within that similarity, you will realize that there is always an "elsewhere," a "somewhere else."

JT What about all of this in relation to your boat, for instance? (Untitled [Sailboat], 1997) (fig. 7a) Here is an object that you basically went out and bought, and then presented pretty much as-is.[9] How does that object operate in relation to the others?

JP It's a small sailboat built in Santa Cruz by this eccentric designer, Bill Lee, who decided to rewrite all the rules of sailing for racing— it's all about speed. The boat is a work that sometimes I think is interesting, sometimes not. I found the boat while I was trying to deal with this big project exhibition at the MCA in Chicago, and I wanted to see if I could get somebody to look at something nine times, by having a different show in the gallery each week (*Jorge Pardo*, January 25–April 13, 1997) (fig. 7b). I wanted to propose the boat almost like a camera in the sense that, every time the show would change, the boat would stay there, and you would begin to set up a relationship between what was in the gallery and this boat. In a way, the boat was the thing that actually started to investigate the subject; it started to lend a potential interpretation to what was going on outside it.

JT   **Could you see the exhibition through the boat?**

JP   No. At least, not literally ... You'd come in and see this boat in an atrium. One week there would be a show of my nephew's drawings; and then the next week there would be a show of the walls painted pink; and then the walls would be painted yellow; and then there was a show of glues, different kinds of glues, produced in the Chicago area; and then at a certain point, around the fourth or fifth week, all the shows were resumed, but in reverse order, until the whole thing collapsed in on itself.

JT   **How did you choose what would be shown each time?**

JP   It really didn't matter ...

JT   **... Just so long as the shows were different enough from each other?**

JP   Yeah, but again, what didn't matter was the specific *meaning* of those differences. Because, initially, there might have been some sort of proximity between the shows and the boat—like, some of the materials comprising the boat would actually manifest themselves in the shows. But then, others wouldn't, and ultimately it became absurd to even try to relate these things ... At the same time, I was trying to unload the boat of all these stupid thoughts having to do with sailing. I mean, I was trying to empty out the

9   This description is not entirely accurate, for only the hull was purchased "as is." The artist then proceeded to refurbish the boat, adding a coat of paint, reconstructing the cabin, supplying it with a mast and sail, etc. However, Pardo emphasizes that these incursions were aesthetically "minimal." Essentially, his aim was to restore the boat to working order.

maritime space of the boat by making it subject to things it had no familiarity with, just to see what would happen. In a way, it is one of the most traditional works of art I have ever made. It's, like, "I like this thing, now what can I do with it?" I just brought it into the show and started doing stuff to it. And, like I said, it was kind of a failure…

JT   You got this sense from talking with people?

JP   Yeah. There was just too much distance there between what a viewer was asked to project and the ultimate payoff—maybe there just wasn't enough payoff. *I* thought it was relatively successful, but what that work really made clear to me is that it doesn't matter what you deal with in terms of objects, materials or ideas, or in terms of how you relate all these things, but the work has to produce a known payoff.

JT   But, structurally speaking, I would think that the fact that you came full-circle with the show, and ended up right where you began, that in itself would seem to provide some sort of payoff or resolution.

JP   I was thinking about a [Robert] Smithson sculpture, one of his mirror corner pieces, and how beautifully it leans into the wall and then just folds in on itself. And I was thinking about how this kind of structure might function in relation to these other sorts of ideas about maritime space, the boat, Chicago, and so on. I was very surprised, in the end, that I could still articulate something about symmetry within a project like that.

JT   The boat is an object that you can reuse, and right now it's on its way to Royal Festival Hall in London where it is going to do—what? (*Jorge Pardo: Untitled*, May 13–July 4, 1999) (fig. 7b)

JP   I don't know. I think that the boat will just be the boat in this case.

JT   So you're leaving some room open for the boat to be affected by the specificities—the contingencies—of that space? Isn't it going to be presented on its side?

JP   Yeah. It doesn't fit upright. The ceiling there is twenty-some feet—which is pretty high—but then the boat is thirty-seven feet. So we're going to have to turn it.

3

THE POETIC AND THE SINISTER

TRANSPARENCY

AESTHETIC AND ECONOMIC VALUES

ASSIMILATION

L.A. ART AND CRITICISM

CRAFT

Los Angeles
c. 1999–2002

Here, we return to the dual nature of Jorge's practice. Some time before we began taping our conversations, he mentioned to me that his work is comprised of a "poetic" as well as a "sinister" side—a description that stuck with me. We tend to think of poetry as an opening up, and perhaps even an emancipation of language, but that is to overlook the element of control that lurks within it, both with regard to what is done to the language and what it does to us. If we can think of art as a language, then for this Cuban-born artist with a working-class background it would have to be a second language, much like his English. "How does a person like me make art?" he asks rhetorically in the course of this discussion, implying that he is someone for whom the lingua franca will always remain to some extent foreign, but also that this is exactly how he wants it. The topic of assimilation is examined under a critical light, yet no iron-clad identity is asserted on the other side of it. Rather, identity, in Pardo's work, is always under negotiation—which also accounts for its potentially sinister aspect. The mention of the artist Kevin Appel further on suggests to me that this conversation occurred in early 2000, around the time of the closing of Appel's MOCA Focus exhibition.

JT I wanted to talk about the dialectic between what you term the "poetic" and the "sinister" poles of your practice. There is a way that you structure the experience of reception so that one goes from consuming the work to being consumed by it. You also mentioned the possibility of taking pleasure in one's own consumption by the work.

JP Yeah, I think that anytime you become attracted to something, it's always about overcoming a kind of deficit... Like, if you drive by a building each day, it's going to take some kind of sinister act to make you take notice and reevaluate it aesthetically. It's aggressive: there's been a shift, and the inconsequential has suddenly become consequential. It doesn't just happen. It takes a kind of aggression to make you change the way you perceive.

JT This is related to control…

JP …A manipulation of some sort. And I don't think that the more traditional Marxist model applies here, you know, where manipulation is bad unless you're sharing the wealth. You can just be manipulated because of the way that it feels aesthetically. The idea of productivity exists in this whole other realm in this case; this has nothing to do with economics. When I was in school, you made works that allowed you to see what the problem was. There was always this very strong Marxist tendency, and you really had to be clear about your position.

JT You're talking about a kind of transparency: signaling your position, your political allegiances, from miles away. So there's no point in the work where anyone risks losing their footing.

JP Right. It's kind of a mythic relation to transparency. It's mythic just to think that you can control reception to that degree. Generally, transparency, real transparency, is much more fucked up than that. Real transparency is not about "good things." There's a price you pay for it in that you are made to see the most horrible… It positions you in an entirely ambivalent space. It's almost the opposite of what we were talking about earlier as Marxist. Transparency does not equal consciousness.

JT You're talking about a real transparency as opposed to Marxist transparency or the art world's version, say.

JP I think that those are both related.

JT Well, the art world's transparency, as far as I can tell, has to do with establishing some sort of clear connection between the viewer and maker of the work. In that sense, all the cards are laid out on the table.

JP But that translates directly into the Socialist model also. There, transparency is all about being able to count the money, to provide a full accounting—where did it go, how was it spent, who got it, who didn't? It's the same thing, really; it's just a question of an aesthetic itinerary versus an economic one. It just becomes perverse, and the problems become more explicit to me, when it is used in an art context. Because there is no good reason to administrate the meaning of the work in this way. It doesn't make anything interesting happen. Whereas if you're dealing with GNP in relation to the minimum wage, for instance, it makes a lot of sense.

JT Wouldn't you agree, though, that there is this tendency—and I see it as much in your work as what you say about it—to translate aesthetic concepts into concepts of value—that is to say, economic value.

JP Absolutely. I think that those terms are so much more efficient. But at the same time, I'm very conscious of aligning myself with a poetic, versus a much more pragmatic take on things. I don't think that artworks necessarily benefit from the fact that the artist is honest, or eager to put everything out there in a way that tallies up. I don't think that one has to be fully in control of the situation. Artworks are much more interesting when the opportunity arises for the experiential to become much more monstrous, much more baroque. The artworks that I'm interested in are ones that build structures that I can't really deal with, or that have no problem operating with a very high degree of ambivalence, let's say, in regard to what the work is, what it's trying to do, how it's failing, how it's not...

JT I see what you're saying. It seems to me that this remains one of the principal privileges of art: that it can, in fact, maintain that sort of position, and do so in relation to other sorts of artifacts, other sorts of goods, that are very clear as to their function and purpose. In art, questions of investment or interest can always be suspended, or deferred...

JP ...Or, in fact, the motive of the artwork can be to create an uncomfortable space for the viewer.

JT I think what's interesting is that, right from the outset, when aesthetics was first connected to the idea of interest, or rather *disinterest*, that connection directly implied an economy, money...

The idea, right from the start, was to somehow separate the beautiful from the merely valuable—or, again, from money. That's just where modern aesthetics comes from.

JP Basically, the reason we did that, I would assume, is so that art could never be currency. It would have to exist in this whole other realm. In other words, it's so that it could be manipulated to a much higher degree.

JT There's a defensive side to formalism. It's like how advertising often deals right up front with our main objection to the proposed product. You know, like how that slogan "soup is good food" serves to counter the objection that soup might not be food at all, that it might just be a drink or something. What the ad is saying is that this can of Campbell's is not a soda—even though it might look like one—it's a whole meal. In art, also, we're dealing with the problem right off the bat—the problem of currency, of commodification—because, in a way, artworks are the ultimate commodities, pure exchange value.

JP It's in the way that an artwork can synthesize all of the oppositions within a given social system. Then you're actually making something incredibly fucked up. Then every evaluative condition of the aesthetic becomes perverse. I don't know why you would want to do something like that.

JT Especially in this culture it seems like such an odd move.

JP I don't know. I think it's probably a class issue. There's very little art out there that's been made by people who aren't either middle or upper class. I'd like to think that I'm working to understand that problem. And it's not necessarily because I believe that the problem is some sort of ideological hurdle to overcome, but simply because I'm not from that culture, so again the question comes down to: how does a person like me make art? That's really where all of these problems come from. Just the fact that they are problems, that I ask these questions, or that these questions are asked of me, in so many different ways—and not just rhetorically, but in the way that certain conventions are strange to me because I don't quite understand them; or in the way I perceive them as limits, places I can't go; or in the way that, when I do finally make something, there's going to be a measure of vulgarity in it—that's the way all this stuff makes itself manifest in my thought and my work. It's an interesting problem because, in the end, it's not really worthwhile to make art for anybody but yourself. And I'm not about to start making art about mobility or anything like that. Everyone is still running around with this idea that America is one of the most mobile places in the world, but really it isn't. There is no black art in America; there is no feminism; there's only art. I mean, the highest aspiration that one can have is just this generalization, this assimilation.

JT   So, you're saying that your work is about reading this existing system or structure—this culture, basically—but from the position of an outsider ... At least, that's part of it, right?

JP   It's about reading, but also wanting to participate, in a sense; or to participate, but with real implications. Like, I would like to see what happens when you make a work of art that really constipates the things that are supposed to make it move.

JT   I've thought a lot about this, and it strikes me that so much of what you make exists in this incredibly complex socially coded system. Just to understand this system on some surface level is itself a major feat, I think. To understand how different classes signify their positions, how they speak to each other by either tucking in their shirts or not—you know, all these minute nuances of dress and pose—is not an easy thing. It seems like you've almost thrown yourself into this enormously difficult "system of objects," as [Jean] Baudrillard puts it, and on one level, you're simply reading it, whereas on another level, you're actively playing with it too. But just to read it, I'm saying, is a feat.

JP   I don't know. I think that there's an ambiguity in what I'm doing where you can't really read it, but at the same time you realize that reading it isn't really enough. I want ...

JT   ... But you were the one to bring it up: the fact that class is the big secret of American life.

JP   Absolutely, it's this thing that's not supposed to exist. Take Hollywood: it's all based on class. The origins of the Jewish community within Hollywood, which was rife with antisemitism, is particularly interesting.

JT But what this makes for is a very complex system of signification...

JP ...It's almost allegorical.

JT It is, but the actual signifiers of class become more and more minute and slight and subtle because, as you said, they're really not supposed to exist.

JP They're supposed to disappear. There's a whole machinery in place for dissolving class distinctions, but in reality, it doesn't dissolve them; the opposite happens. In fact, the more you try to assimilate, the less successful you are (*laughs*).

JT It's a Kafkaesque scenario.

JP It's entirely Kafkaesque. It's such a purely sinister and sadomasochistic kind of position.

JT Well, that's where I become interested in your idea about consciously doing it wrong, consciously messing up, because there is always a class aspect to these maneuvers, right? On the one hand, you produce a range of high-end luxury items that are modeled on a class of goods that actually exist out there in the world. But then, on the other hand, you also take the opportunity to mess with them somehow, to screw them up formally. So, there is some kind of double-articulation taking place there.

JP There is always this structure within the object that wants to set up a particular sort of reflexivity. The excess in the work is in the service of reflexivity; it's not the other way around, you see? Because excess is typically in service to the rarefication of the thing, you know what I'm saying? We live in a time when works of art have to include reflexivity, but they have to include it in a way where its potency is completely disarmed. In the end, they are not really being reflexive at all. Instead there's a kind of *cozy* reflexivity that is still very necessary for the experience to be complete.

JT Right, it's a kind of status-by-association reflexivity.

JP Exactly, and that takes us right into the problems of someone like Kevin Appel's work.[10] That's a kind of practice where you're not quite sure if it's progressive because it is totally indifferent to these sorts of questions, or if it's incredibly conservative because it doesn't even know they exist. I mean, if his work is about a kind of resistance to these art world orthodoxies then it's potentially interesting. The real issue for me, though, is that you can't tell.

JT This has to do with the so-called zeitgeist. I mean, it wasn't so long ago that you had to be absolutely clear, as an artist, about your position in the work, and this was signaled as self-reflexivity. What you're talking about now is a kind of pseudo-reflexivity that has become the norm. There is an assumption, whenever this sort of content is broached, that the work will be critically reflexive. But often it isn't, really.

JP I think that's very problematic because interesting art, just like interesting criticism, should be involved with changing the way things are. For instance, I would like, when somebody leaves my work, that they have a model for looking at other works that is not the same one they came in with. It's the main reason I got interested in art in the first place, because it's a space where you can actually affect the way that we perceive reality. You can change it on a structural level.

JT Right. But for this reason exactly I can't help but think about how your work has been received in L.A. There's almost a consensus among critics out here that your work is not even remotely critical, that it's totally complicit, totally playing by the rules. How do you account for this response?

JP You're right, it is the dominant reading. I don't know... It's unfortunate.

10 We are discussing Kevin Appel because his work was on view at the time, or had recently closed. Appel mounted his MOCA Focus exhibition between September 26, 1999 and January 2, 2000, shortly after Pardo's *4166 Sea View Lane* project. There were some notable points of intersection between these two exhibitions. While Appel's consisted strictly of paintings, they had to do with architecture and décor. The artist had produced a series of paintings on the basis of a digitally rendered, imaginary glass house, and these were then hung on the walls of the gallery in such a way to afford the audience a 360-degree view of the structure. I had written an essay for the accompanying catalogue, which is maybe another reason we are discussing this show.

JT How do you explain the fact that those same critics that who like to shoot you down can then go on to champion someone like Kevin Appel? I only bring him up because there is a relation there in terms of content, both of you being interested in questions of architecture, the house. And the same can be said for Jim Iserman who is also a favorite among local critics, and sometimes proposed as a kind of positive counter-model to your own practice.

JP Well, both of these artists are involved in this very streamlined sort of production. For instance, I know Jim, and I know that he is interested primarily in the *making* of the object.

JT Something about how that work is made makes it impossible to think about anything other than how it's made. In that sense it is successful, I guess...

JP ...It's basically church work, but interesting. I've always liked Jim's work, especially early on when he would make things he could not afford or maybe did not have access to.

JT Yes, it's tied into that whole Protestant American thing. There's a relation, there, between a certain kind of humble aestheticism and the work ethic...

JP ...It's complicated hand-work.

JT Isn't it amazing that we're still going on about the crafting of these things? How great it is that the artist has learned these skills and makes everything by hand, and so on—that any of this matters?

JP It's mind-boggling actually! It's totally mind-boggling! We haven't lived in that world for a hundred years—maybe never (*laughs*).

JT There's almost been a conscious decision to turn back the clock...

JP ...It's not even about going back because what we're talking about is actually *prehistoric*; it's pre-anthropological—the least reflexive way of looking at things imaginable.

JT It seems like the less the artist is trying to do, the better chance they have of doing it, and doing it successfully, out here. Again, it's like we are back to this modernist model of works divulging their entire substance in a single brief instant...

JP ...Which is something that Jim Iserman's works are actually able to do, over and over...

JT ...Because, if they can't do that, then the experience becomes somehow too ponderous, too taxing, and basically of no consequence. The work gets trashed.

JP I think that it's kind of sad, but not really, because it's always been this way.

JT What's sad about it is that L.A. is actually a very sophisticated place. It's got the highest education levels among artists, but then there's a massive disconnect between that and the gallery system, the system of critical evaluation—the whole professional art world, basically, which responds to a very different set of priorities.

JP But that's really a myth. Maybe there's an educational forum here that is attractive to some people who are interested in looking at things with a certain intensity, but generally speaking, most artists don't actually give much thought to any of the things we're talking about. Very few people—looking at this culture in general—are interested in thinking this way. What you have here is a structure that is set up to educate you "well," just like a finishing school. So, what you have are these very sophisticated finishing schools, and their job is to make sure that everyone can communicate—not just communicate, but to communicate and exploit. Basically, they sell you a kind of identity, a cultural identity, and it comes through critical theory or whatever you want. But, in the end, there is such an absolute break that happens there between this theoretical framework and the substance of your everyday life. It renders the most consequential writing of the last thirty or so years totally irrelevant. Artists aren't really taught about the actual effects of what they are doing, or how it works in the world. Again, there's a degree of aestheticization...

JT Well, the aesthetic, aestheticism, remains absolutely central out here—and I mean by this a kind of modernist, autonomous aesthetics. Because, in actuality, aesthetic questions are interesting only if they impinge on a whole range of other questions—social, political, or whatever. Aesthetics is where those questions can become concrete, in a sense.

JP   Absolutely. Those sorts of questions are interesting when they are about causes. You're trying to understand how a particular effect happens, how it is produced. In that sense, I would say that most of the work that comes out of L.A. isn't even about aesthetics. It would be interesting to find out what exactly it is about. Maybe some sort of issue-driven identity thing…

JT   You're right, there's a whole legacy out here of precisely this sort of professionalized outsider art: artists who are involved in a wide range of extraneous pursuits and concerns, from comic books to rock music. Nothing wrong with that, obviously, but very often this stuff isn't even treated to any kind of mediation, or translation into the terms of art.

JP   I always wondered, when I was going to school here, what exactly I was being trained for. What was I supposed to do as an artist? What was I supposed to look at for inspiration?

JT   The thing that is so odd about the kind of art education that we experienced out here is that art history really wasn't such a big part of it.

JP   And that's probably the best part of it (*laughs*).

4

ARTISTS AND
ARCHITECTS
THE CLIENT RELATION
THE UNFINISHED
PAINTING AND
BUILDING
THE HOUSE AND
ITS VIEW

Los Angeles
c. 1999–2002

In 1998, the architects Linda Taalman and Alan Koch, who together ran a studio named OpenOffice, began to solicit projects from working artists for livable homes that could be reproduced in editioned multiples. I had learned of this project from one of the participating artists some years later, while its production was in full swing, and automatically assumed that Jorge would have been included in their roster, which was not the case. Why not is what he proceeds to explain in this conversation, which serves to further clarify his aesthetic relation to architecture. In short, it does not come down to a simple rejection of function in favor of play, but rather a playful incursion into the processes through which function is determined. A key phrase uttered here is "the client relation." If, in these years, Jorge would find a welcome place among the artists associated with relational aesthetics it is probably due to the fact that his client relations were increasingly incorporated into the physiognomy of his work. In a later conversation, we discuss this in terms of portraiture—that is, as a representation of both the client and the artist.

JT   Let's talk about that OpenOffice project, *TRESSPASSING: Houses x Artists*, and the necessity that you've mentioned on a number of occasions of maintaining some kind of friction between the practices of art and architecture, or design.[11]

JP   I think there's something problematic about the implied mutuality of the OpenOffice invitation, this suggestion that it will benefit both sides equally. It's like when Disney makes movies for adults;

11   In 2003, OpenOffice mounted two back-to-back exhibitions at the MAK Center for Art and Architecture titled *TRESPASSING: Houses x Artists*, which consisted mainly of the plans and models that had been submitted. The first of these exhibitions (January 29–April 13) included work by Jim Iserman, Renée Petropoulos, Jessica Stockholder, and T. Kelly Mason. The second (May 7–July 27) included work by Kevin Appel, Chris Burden, Barbara Bloom, Julian Opie, and David Reed.

it's just that sort of problem. For some reason, architecture wants to engage with the aesthetic, but in a way that really has nothing to do with the aesthetic. So, it approaches it in the way that's most direct: "Oh, let's invite artists to do it, to actually design our houses, and that will be our project!" Maybe there's nothing wrong with that. Maybe it's an interesting situation, but I'm doubtful.

JT Well, it seems that, in California at least, the friction is real. Isn't there an ongoing battle, out here, of artists against architects over that meager one percent allotment for the arts that every new public building is supposed to have? Architects have tended to keep that money for themselves, which generates all kinds of resentment.

JP Another problem that comes to mind is that, when you enter into a project like this, you get a certain kind of result, a certain kind of house, out of it. You won't get a lousy shack, for instance, because there is such a level of idealism at work here that most of the decisions that get made probably won't be that interesting. What's most interesting about a situation like this to me just won't be allowed to surface. You won't be able to articulate any of the problems that occur to people who are actually trying to build houses for people to live in. And at the same time, the architects who are using artists to gain a distance that is necessary for their work to be reflexive—in a way that it couldn't be reflexive on its own—that's just false.

JT Couldn't we conceive of different sorts of reflexivity?

JP Well, then the problem is that when OpenOffice invites artists to build houses, they don't really risk anything. Their categorical status remains intact; their legitimacy as architects is never questioned. It's all too easy.

JT For starters, they do away with the client relation, right?

JP There is no client, and that's one of the most interesting things about architecture. Unfortunately, architects think it's the most limiting thing, but, for my money, the most interesting thing you can do in this situation is to set yourself up a limit of some kind that is astronomical and insurmountable, and then still make something happen in spite of that. In that sense, architecture is not all that different from what you do when you're painting a picture. But very few people understand this. Generally speaking, architects work in this way: they have an idea, it's pure, it goes to the client, the client corrupts the idea, and it's no longer pure, it's no longer interesting, it's no longer theirs. And that's the biggest bullshit imaginable, but that's because architects tend to work in this purely idealistic sort of space.

JT And you're saying that what's wrong with this OpenOffice project is that it just evades to the problem as opposed to claiming it, working with it. But what about in your case? There, the client is essentially you, right?

JP The client is not a client; the architecture is not architecture; the work is not the work. The work is problematic, and it wants to engage that problematic. The client becomes the viewer, in a sense.

JT The client becomes the artist who becomes a viewer, and this in turn allows every viewer to become the artist, in a way. There is a move-ment of give and take between the artist and the viewer—in the house just like in any painting, as you just said. But because it is a house and a home, doesn't that encourage a more socially oriented sort of expe-rience, or reading? Doesn't it, again, partly devolve upon questions of class and status, for instance?

JP There has got to be a way to install measures in the work that make it impossible or unproductive to evaluate the work on these terms— that is, whether the client, or the artist, is a dandy or not, or whether he's poor or he's wealthy—none of that should matter. That's the most conservative way to access a work of art. It's like saying, "I'm interested in this picture, but I will only go on looking at it if the artist is a good person, and if, you know, politically, historically, and so on, they toe the line." The aesthetic culture that I see myself involved in is very much amoral.

JT When you talk about maintaining a non-idealistic position in respect to your house, I think about how you structure the experience of reception, of moving through it.

JP I'm talking about a way to consume it, or to perceive it—and not even *it*, but the world. It's a way to perceive the configuration of decisions that are being made, and that, together, constitute a world. It's a system of relations, ultimately, that link up the buildings, the exhibitions in the buildings, what I'm doing there before or after ... I'd like to do something different in that space every day because I want to avoid ever getting to that point of refinement. It's idealistic. I don't want the work to be thought of as something finished; I want to avoid that sort of idealism at any cost. I mean, I have been making a lot of objects, for the last five or six years or longer, that maybe reuse similar materials or ideas in similar ways, but if you actually look at the work, and at the kinds of decisions that make up the work, I think you'd be surprised at just how uncomplementary it all is in the end.

JT Well, it seems to me that, in certain instances, you're very conscious about structuring the viewer's experience of your work as something unfinished or, as you say, "uncomplementary." Like in that show at the MCA in Chicago, where you move all the component parts of the installation around from one week to the next: that seems like a direct attempt to undermine one's expectations, let's say, for a certain kind of constancy and coherence. At the level of reception, then, you wind up with these two very different sorts of readings. There are those viewers who return and see the unfolding of the work over time, and then there are those who only come once, and for them, it's somewhat more constant, maybe. But, in actuality, they are only getting a small part of it, a fragment.

JP I think that, if a viewer only gets a small part of it, I'd welcome that sort of corruption. I think it's a given, this partial view of things. To talk about a work of art as having any sort of stability is just something I can't understand. To make a work that produces a consistent set of effects—why bother?

JT But this is one of the ways in which things are understood: they have to taken out of context and, in a sense, shut down. And, in art especially, it would seem that the whole support structure of it—from the reviews to the catalogues and the retrospective exhibitions—all of it functions to somehow finish the work. These things serve to insert a series of almost arbitrary pauses into the unfolding of the artist's career; they tell us when it's finished, when it's ready to be looked at, when it's ready to be thought about, talked about, and so on. And I see your work, in this regard, as being very conscious and strategic about thwarting those structures that want to close art down.

JP Yeah. That's one of the things that makes contemporary art boring: it turns you into a kind of specialist. On the other hand, though, what's interesting about contemporary art is that you can actually take charge of the limits of your practice versus its fruitfulness, let's say. You know, you can propose to simply make problems instead of providing any sort of solution.

JT One thing that's clear is that you're very much oriented, in your practice, toward problems of reception...

JP ...But every artist is.

JT I don't know about that.

JP What's different about my work is that it gives you problems. It sort of constipates your experience, it delineates it. It makes it very difficult to say why any one thing is better than any other.

JT Well, maybe you're right in saying that every artist is interested in reception, but maybe not the *problems* of reception—that's something else. I mean, reception is where you want to make contact, connections, right? And, in that sense, I see what you're doing as inherently risky, because you're constantly risking a kind of misreading, basically.

JP I don't think that works of art can be misread, actually.

JT OK, OK, but...

JP ...There's a general level of arbitrariness in this culture, and what I'm trying to do is to understand that and maximize that. If artworks are not exactly what we think they are, if they are so susceptible to corruption, then I'd like to make that point manifest in their structure, their intent. Because nothing in this world is ever done. No painting, for instance, is ever done, and when you look at things in this way, you see just how fucked up they really are. Basically you're just dealing with scraps, with billions of incomplete fragments.

The conversation resumes after a break and we conclude it at 4166 Sea View Lane.

JP   Back to Appel, if the work comes out of painting, it makes perfect sense that he wants to build a glass house. That, to me, is something to wrestle with. Now, what's potentially interesting about this work is that it makes it impossible for us to gauge his distance from the subject. But all that could be getting lost now because, ultimately, it's all about transparency. And I don't think that he's dealing with transparency in a reflexive way; it's not about the problems of transparency …

JT   … It's more like an analogy of the problem is what you're saying.

JP   It's more like an ornament on the problem, or something … For example, what I'd like my own work to do is this: if someone comes to it wanting to know what my relationship to modernism is, then they'd be able to know that. And not because of empathy or some sort of projection, but because I'm still trying to analyze my own relationship to those kinds of questions.

JT   Actually, I think that Appel is more invested in questions pertaining to the image, and to the technical relations between painted images and photographed images, and so on. So, that's basically how he lays claim to this modernist content. His investigation of architectural space—if that's what we agree to call it—is very specific to its various representations, and to how these are affected by the inception of different visual technologies.

JP   But on a fundamental level, the way that this work actually operates is very much unlike what you've just described.

JT   Well, yes, because it is painting and because, as painting, it's going to be not only about space, but also surface, facture. And that's maybe what's successful about this painting—like most probably any successful painting—its ability to negotiate these very different sorts of experiences in a way that's convincing and, at the same time, surprising.

JP   …

JT   ... This painterly aspect, though, that's something that you're dealing with as well—at least, that's the sense I get. So many of the decisions you're making in regard to your house are painterly decisions—like, in the bathroom, the color of the tiles next to the color of the grout. You've tinted the grout so that it's functioning almost like something out of a paint tube.

JP   But it's bigger than that because, generally, when people think about a space to live in, there isn't that sort of malleability—you know, like, let's take down this wall because we want to see what it looks like on the other side of the room. That's antithetical, basically, to what a house is. A house is about stability, protecting people, and so on. In that sense, the painterly gesture *inside* a house is a very eccentric proposition, but that's the relationship to painting I'm interested in. I'm interested in the possibility of taking the purely aesthetic and inserting it into places where it's going to be more than just perverse.

JT   You're engaging the aesthetic in a literally concrete sense.

JP   Well, yeah, because when you take this wall out, for instance, the room feels bigger.

JT   You're adding a practical dimension to the aesthetic.

JP   Right.

JT   But there's no conclusion to any of this. You've actually built in this structure where the work must evolve over a long time.

JP   It just ended up that way ... Because that's the way I am.

JT   But, also, you want the process, the amount of time that it takes, to pull you off-track, right? In regard to any sort of original plan? Isn't that part of its whole, as you say, "anti-idealistic" aspect?

JP   It just seems to make sense. If you don't have enough money to bring it off at one time, you know, how do you make that work for you? How can that limit begin to structure your project? But it's not always like that. I'm working on a couple of houses right now (fig. 8 and fig. 9) where it can't be like that, because, there, taking one's time would cost a fortune.[12] So it's not a consistent architectural strategy or anything like that. I just wanted to make those things clear in one particular work—all the limits that I face financially, aesthetically, experientially...

JT   ... These are all the, again, "contingencies" that you are here manifesting in a very intentional way. I mean, they are built into your project—and maybe any project—almost arbitrarily, but then you choose to claim them emphatically as elements of your process.

JP   The way you respond to them actually initiates the intentionality of the process.

JT   Now, it seems to me that the house on Sea View Lane is very clear about your ambivalence vis-à-vis the viewer. Because of its structure—it has a kind of "shotgun" layout that's been bent—there is only one way to move through it. It directs the viewer in a very forceful way. But then, at the same time, I know that you want to resist any kind of totalizing reading or take, any sort of coherent...

JP   ... Actually, it has eleven doors. I mean, if you treat it like a circuit, sure, but generally speaking, the way the house actually gets used is very different. Like, today, for instance, you came in by way of the stairs, through the studio; but, other times, you'll come in through the kitchen. I usually come in through the bedroom. So, it's actually very difficult to have this unilateral traffic you're talking about. It just doesn't happen.

JT   Well, the first time I saw it—I think it might have been on the day it first opened to the public—I came through with a pretty sizable audience, and we all started out at one end and then worked our way to the other end. And, at that time, I really had the sense that the house was almost like an architectural ride. I remember telling you that. The way it seems to exaggerate all these intrinsically architectural experiences—you know, all the sudden shifts in scale and perspective: a room suddenly narrows, or turns into a plunging stairway—it runs through the whole gamut by the time you

12   One of these houses is the private home of Cesar and Mimma Reyes in Naguabo, Puerto Rico (completed in 2005), and the other is a guesthouse compound for visitors and artists-in-residence at the Krabbesholm Højskole in Skive, Denmark (completed in 2006).

come out the other end. It really did feel like a ride because there was this programmed aspect to it, and this long line of people shuttling through.

JP Alright…

JT …And even those things you're talking about that disrupt that kind of movement, even there, I get the sense that you're conscious of them as disruptions, precisely. You're conscious of how, when you enter through the kitchen, for instance, how that's a disruption of some underlying pattern. So, in that sense, I think that it works to emphasize all those decisions that we make on our own, right? Because they go against the grain?

JP Yeah, absolutely. That's why it's all connected from one room to the next. In a sense, the hallway's outside. That was the most interesting way to deal with that land before there was a house there. I remember walking around on that property and thinking that it was interesting to walk this way. Because you have a view, but then you also don't have a view. In the house, there are no external windows, or very few, that look outside; mostly they look in on a big courtyard garden. So when you look out the house, you're inside. That's what was so interesting about the lot: that it manifested such a polymorphous sort of relationship to itself, to its terrain.

JT So you walked through the lot, and then you based your design of the house on that early experience you had of the land, before there was anything built on it?

JP Pretty much. Why not keep all those features in there that are specific to the land? That was a big part of the thinking around that project. And the other part was: how do you disrupt that relation, you know, for the sake of reflexivity? But then, also: how do you gain reflexivity without completely eliminating those relationships? How do you bring it in in a more functional way, let's say, by way of those functional contaminates that inevitably come in to corrupt our experience.

JT I think it is enormously provocative, the way you're talking about all this, and because of the way that time is brought into the experience: the idea of a work changing over time, never reaching completion. The way that you're basically protracting the whole production process so that every time you come back, you see something different.

JP   It's like any house in that sense.

JT   Except that it's not a house, or not "only" a house, right?

JP   Right.

Fig. 5 Jorge Pardo, *Untitled (¼" Scale, Counter, Bank of America, Altadena, California)*, 1999.

Fig. 6 *Pier*, 1997. Installation view, Skulptur Projekte Münster.

Fig. 7a *Untitled (Sailboat)*, 1997. Installation view, Queen Elizabeth Hall, Southbank Centre, London (1999).

Fig. 7b *Untitled (Sailboat)*, 1997. Installation view Museum of Contemporary Art, Chicago.

5

ABOUT OUR CONVERSATION

ROMANTICISM AND PUNK ROCK

RUINS

THE COMRADE AND THE SERF

Los Angeles
October 23, 2002

Prior to this meeting, which took place over lunch, Jorge and I had decided that we would publish our conversations in book form, but then the question was immediately raised as to what sort of book it should be. More specifically, since we had at this point agreed to keep talking together indefinitely, the question came down to this: How could one keep a book from offering a summation—from delivering the last word, so to speak—since this is precisely what books tend to do? Our exchange on this point would typically have been edited out of a more conventional artist interview, yet here it is left in as a nod to our original aims. As it turns out, this book has assumed a somewhat orthodox format, yet hopefully there remains in it some sense of the effect of time on talk, the ebb and flow of sustained interpersonal communication, that we had initially made out as the most compelling quality of this project. Appropriately, on this day—the first conversation to be properly dated—our discursive parameters are especially broad; the discussion drifts from art to music to communism. What might tie these various topics together is a mutual interest in what remains incommensurable between human experience and its expression.

JT   After I talked to you about the idea of putting out our conversation as a book, it occurred to me that the book could be in volumes, ostensibly.

JP   Yeah, you just keep going.

JT   Exactly. Maybe there's some way to suggest that it actually does not come to any kind of conclusion, at any point.

JP   It would also be interesting if it could witness a reversal of positions. Have it be something that, you know, is not reducible to any kind of ideological position, that does the complete opposite, in that it loops, or something like that.

JT   So there's the possibility of maybe returning to certain ideas later.

JP   Yes. [Suddenly, everyone in the restaurant where we are seated is talking much more loudly.] We've created an enthusiasm all around! That's fortunate.

JT   That's very true ... There's a book by Martin Kippenberger that is basically the model for me.[13] It's constructed around an interview that's so rambling, so inclusive and seemingly unedited, that it does some of the things we are talking about. Obviously, I think it could be taken further, especially with this idea of volumes.

JP   I know the book, but I've never gone through it.

JT   I have just an edited version of it. I know that he put out books periodically, and that was one of them. And I think he interspersed photographs semi-arbitrarily, and I think that the interview was presented as continuous, the whole thing. Ours would be different in that sense. But I love the idea that it would really take place over many years. Maybe at some point we could fabricate cases for our volumes, that they would fit snugly inside of? Thinking ahead, we could have some kind of consistent aesthetic, or we could even come up with an imprint, or something that would give it a consistent look.

JP   I tend to want to take the other track: I'd like to have them be as disparate as possible. And the reason I am interested in using images is because they're sort of anti-organizational. They propose a resistance to this notion that thought is something that could be structured. It would be nice to completely shift the aesthetic of the books from one to the other, but still maintain the thrust ... you know what I mean?

13   This in reference to the artist's book, *B – Gespräche mit Martin Kippenberger* (Ostfildern: Hatje Cantz Verlag, 1994). This book consists of four long conversations carried out between Kippenberger and Jutta Koether in 1990 and 1991 in Cologne, Frankfurt, and on a train. These were recorded and then transcribed directly, without correction or any kind of editorial imposition on the flow of talk. The model for Kippenberger, announced upfront in the title, is obviously Andy Warhol's 1968 "telephone book," *a: A Novel*.

JT   So there might be a relation between one book and the next, and then another relation between that and the next book...

JP   It'll be the information that holds it together.

JT   This is one of the reasons that I think of Kippenberger as the model figure in this case. It's surprising to me, considering that he did do quite a bit of work out here in L.A., how little that model seems to have been acted upon. I think he's an artist who was very conscious of the fact that meaning comes to his work through all these different channels and contexts that often exist outside of the work—like the book, the catalogue, the interview, the anecdote, or the rumor even. All of these things are sort of external, not intrinsic to the art object. Today, again, we seem to be talking about it all coming back around to this autonomous work that can completely generate its own context. But it seems that you've always considered these sorts of external, extraneous kinds of relations in your own work.

JP   I've always assumed that works of art were fragments of things, not even necessarily fragments of a whole or anything as ridiculous as that, but just fragmentary—these fragmentary sorts of propositions in regard to the particular places they inhabit. They're just sorts of ideas that you're sifting through. So I never really thought that my generation could seriously consider the concept of autonomy or maintain anything like that delusional sort of rigor that, you know, my parents had.

JT   Right. So there's kind of an acceptance, I'd say, that works are essentially fragments, and you know that no matter what you do, no matter how whole you want to make these things, that's all they're going to be. So, if you take that into account to begin with, you can start to operate in these various other positions.

JP   I think that the reason that Kippenberger had almost no impact in Los Angeles was that he really *wasn't here.* He just came over with Max Hetzler and Luhring Augustine and a few other art world specialists, and he talked to some kids about the history of the L.A. art scene, and that's about it. What they tried to do with their program was simply to replace their ideological model here.[14] It's just that it happened in a kind of a vacuum...

JT The fact is that, I think, they tried to stake this town out.

JP They tried to make Kippenberger into a big deal: you know, like, "We're opening a gallery in L.A.!" "And Kippenberger's moving out!" And so there's obviously some belief that with somebody like Kippenberger—a big personality, a German—that that sort of charisma can travel. But, in the end it didn't really work because, you know, it's America. We have a completely different demographic structure out here. Kippenberger in Cologne literally had students chasing him around, listening to every word, waiting for assignments.

JT We're also working with a much more positivistic model of how art functions, how it's taught...

JP ...I think that nobody really takes it seriously, that model of the pedagogical. Pedagogy is something that's still a little bit postwar out here; it's still very much influenced by the sixties, by having teachers that, in the end, aren't really that much older than you are. All these sorts of public universities, or open universities, from the sixties and seventies, their influence is still very present. And the same goes for the junior colleges, where you're basically being taught by your peers. That's very different from Germany where teachers maintain these kinds of positions for life. The Germans' pedagogical model is very conservative but, at the same time, it's weird. The line of descent—where who you were a student of and who they were a student of—is very important there, and it produces weirdness. So, you can have a heretic like Kippenberger command a certain kind of following.

JT In the U.S., though, there's an obsession with art theory, which basically comes out of German Romanticism. It seems to me that there's, let's say, two sides to German Romanticism, but then there's just one side that's taken up within American art school pedagogy, and it's the idealistic side. But there's a whole other side that is exactly in line with what you like to talk about: it seizes on the fragment non-idealistically. It's about the idea that meaning can

14 The Luhring Augustine Hetzler gallery had a location in Santa Monica from 1989 to 1992. Its closure was largely blamed on the economic recession, which had a devastating impact on the Los Angeles art scene at the time.

never be whole, that it can only be glimpsed in bits and pieces, that communication can't happen in any holistic way.

JP Give me some examples of artists who maintain that position.

JT I think Kippenberger was very much working in that way. In the end, he comes full circle, and you see that he was working with these Romantic models all along. He resuscitated all these, let's say, ur-Expressionist paintings—like that Raft of the Medusa series he put into one of his last shows—and he wasn't going about it purely ironically.[15] He put his own kind of spin on the proceedings, but ultimately he was reflecting on these same ideas: the idea that the work is something that falls apart, for instance.

JP I think Kippenberger was never really invested in that problem. I see his work, at best, as a kind of a systematic dispersion machine to, like, anything serious—but it is precisely so that he could be serious in the end. The reason Kippenberger was not really interesting to me was that he really was invested in this idea of being serious, which is also why he sort of rolls back into Romanticism. And that's also why he decided to do, you know, the monolithic "fuck you" that comes from punk rock or something like that. The deinstrumentalized "fuck you" that a lot of kids in the States really fetishized.

JT That's true, that's true, but ...

JP ... And I think that his belief in punk as a kind of working mode had to do with setting up a poetic between these two kinds of objects ...

JT ... At once serious and unserious, or serious *because* unserious. Yes, I think that that is a very Romantic position.

15 In 1996, Kippenberger began work on a monumental series of photographs, drawings, lithographs, and paintings all relating to Théodore Géricault's seminal *The Raft of the Medusa* (1819). In his versions, Kippenberger proposes himself as the sole model, essentially reenacting the poses of all the doomed figures on the makeshift raft. This work was exhibited at a number of venues, including Galerie Gisela Capitain and Akademie der Künste in Berlin, in 1997—the year of the artist's death from liver cancer.

JP Punk rock is one of the most Romantic movements in music. It's based on a bunch of little kids running amok in their bedrooms.

JT Right down to the aesthetics of it, and there, again, there's a kind of valuation of the ruin.

JP There's different phases to the aesthetic of it. You know, I don't listen to punk rock records, but I had many friends in college who did. The more interesting ones to me were those who didn't really think about it aesthetically so much.

JT Right. But I'm not really talking about a conscious aesthetic; I'm talking about the fact that a ruined-work concept exists maybe more implicitly at the heart of punk rock. Let's say, for instance, that in punk there's a valuation of a kind of a spirit or energy over and above any kind of training, any kind of technical know-how or skill. So, the idea that you could train yourself to a point of perfection as a musician is dismissed out of hand in favor of these hit-and-miss kinds of situations. You know, either it's going to charge people up or it's going to be a total failure. And every punk rock show operates on that principle. You're not going out to see quality or talent; you're going to feed off a kind of buzz that might not even happen.

JP Right.

JT I think, on that level, it's a very Romantic concept: Romanticism as a proto-avant-garde concept that's intrinsically oriented against conventional notions of skill.

JP Yeah, you're talking about a kind of culture that resurrected these notions of authenticity of presence. One of the reasons we have this model is because it's the only way to reinvent performance … because performance is the only way you can demonstrate presence. I agree with you, but I think that that's just one aspect of it. The other part that I'm more interested in is more about the bankruptcy of that kind of belief system. Because it's almost like a kind of spiritualism, what you're talking about.

JT Right, absolutely. And I agree that there's a very reactionary aspect to it, but there's also this other aspect, which is actually quite interesting, that has to do with, again, a kind of problematic concept of the work. It also operates within the structure of recording, the record. That's almost a clearer context for dealing with these sorts of issues ...

JP ... Because the performance is made copyable, reproducible. It can be made of all of the things that were music before.

JT I'm also talking about how a kind of obsolete or defunct urbanism became the context of punk rock. In downtown L.A., just like in the worst parts of England, there's a kind of ruined industrialism that formed the perfect backdrop for these sorts of records. It's right there on the cover, and it's interesting how the music always seems to occupy this same space.

JP This idea of a ruin: it's not a historical, but a *hysterical* ruin. Because it's sort of like when rich kids from Northern Europe were sent off to Greece and Southern Italy, and they brought back all these columns and friezes and things like that. It's not really any different than that. These are both hopelessly Romantic and spiritually bankrupt positions.

JT But there is also a kind of recycling taking place that maybe serves to mitigate some of that bankruptcy. Because, in a way, the ruin is already bankrupt. So when some punks decide to occupy a disused factory, for instance, they are effectively turning it into something else. Those spaces get freed up; they gain a whole new purpose, even if it's only to act as a backdrop for a performance of some sort.

JP I never think about space as having that kind of a reciprocal function. That's why these classical models are always so problematic: because they always imply a kind of a rebirth or something. And I think that things ... things just happen.

JT It's not really a rebirth because what we're talking about is no longer functional and remains so—it's a ruin. I mean, it's taken up as dysfunctional, obsolete.

JP But it still has the capacity to attract the fetishistic gaze, and everything that's like that gets resurrected. It's not a ruin in the sense that no one knows what it is; it's a ruin that has a very specific kind of historical purpose. For me, what's interesting about punk rock, or rather what's most problematic about it, is also what's most authentic about it.

JT I'm with you there. I believe that we're following the same line of argument.

JP I think that authenticity is always what gets you in the end.

JT That's the problem, I agree, but that's not exactly what I'm talking about. I don't think that there's any kind of authentic access to be gained into any particular moment through the form of its ruins. And I don't think that the ruin can serve to bolster the aura of intensity, or authenticity, or whatever you want, of the performance occurring in front of it now. But I do think that, as a sign system, it can get reformulated in various ways, and that something else can come out of it.

JP I think that I disagree. I don't think that much of anything interesting has come out of punk rock. It's infantile.

JT You know, [Walter] Benjamin has this thing about children: how children always inherit the obsolete object-world of their elders. They get the stuff that doesn't work anymore, basically; they get the broken telephone or TV, or the torn-up boxes they came in; that's what becomes theirs. Benjamin is also responding to the fact that kids love to hang out in building sites and garbage dumps, and how there's always this kind of special relation that they have to things left behind. It's always the most disposable stuff that is the most provocative because, as a kid, you know just how to use it. And this later translates into an attraction to these spaces that are kind of intermediate, transitional—spaces that aren't functional anymore, like these ruins we're talking about. It's interesting in that light, I think, especially, the whole punk rock phenomenon. Because essentially, you're looking at middle-class kids being drawn to the ruins of the working classes—these are literally the ruins of the factory. There is a search for authenticity there, but what actually happens is much more bizarre, even phantasmagoric.

The conversation resumes after a break.

JP We've talked about this before: how the working class is just a total postwar phenomenon. The worker doesn't really mean anything in America, or in the West, unless you have some notion of the "comrade" to build on. When did the unions die? When Reagan came into power and with Russian glasnost, right? With the Eastern bloc falling, why the fuck do you need to pay people to do work? If you're not fighting that war anymore?

JT **Correct me if I'm wrong here, but what's coming to mind is that, around the time of the Russian Revolution, let's say 1917, there wasn't even a working class in Russia. There wasn't even a proletariat in Russia. I mean, the industrial proletariat that Marx writes about hadn't appeared yet. So, there it was a completely imagined, constructed entity right from the outset. In the place where the supposedly authentic version of the comrade congeals, you know, you get a ghost.**

JP You don't have a real comrade until monies from the Second World War are redistributed.

JT **Exactly, exactly.**

JP And then you only have it from, like, 1945 to 1980.

JT **So you have a massive revolution that's being fought on behalf of this imagined constituency.**

JP And also, I mean, Russia's a place that's so big in this century that it can actually do that. But at the same time, its jurisdiction doesn't mean anything; it's so far away that it cannot affect the center.

JT **Right, because the working class is an industrial phenomenon. You don't have an agrarian working class. A farmer isn't a working-class person.**

JP Farmers are indentured.

JT **Right.**

JP The problem with agrarianism is that it's slave labor. It's not necessarily a working class, so what do you do with it? How do you represent the people that actually have to pick your food? And, historically, that's a point of transition because, in the States, there was no kind of revolution for that class of people until the sixties.

JT Well, that's true, I suppose, because, ultimately, they hark back to a feudal structure, to serfdom. I think of Jack Kerouac picking grapes in *On the Road*, and just disappearing, in a way, for a time ...

JP There's no future outside the wall. You come in and work in order to pay for the manors. I think of these different kinds of feudal workers as being almost outside the state. I think of them as slaves because they're outside the humanistic economy. You're not considered human if you're a farmer; you're made for work. The world's always got to have people like that.

JT So, there's no question there of an industrial structure with unions and worker's rights ... or even human rights.

JP Now, the problem with the comrade is that, in order to make money in an industrial society, you have to live very close to the people that you're exploiting. These are not people you want to live next to. I mean, they're just not (*laughs*). You have to clean them up; there's a kind of *maintenance* involved. And then also, you know, if the new domain of the lord is what you're seeing on a daily basis, then you're less inclined to lick the shit off (*laughs*). You know what I mean?

JT You're absolutely right. I don't know if you've had a chance to read Engels on the industrial working class in Britain, in Manchester?[16] It's a fascinating text; it supplies some basis for *Das Kapital* and the *Communist Manifesto*. But the thing that's so stunning about it is the tone, the attitude toward, primarily, questions of hygiene and cleanliness. And I know the argument that's being made is that

16 Friedrich Engels' *The Conditions of the Working Class in England* was written during the two-year period (1842–44) that the author spent managing his father's textile mill in Salford, in the greater Manchester area. His father had reportedly sent him there to temper his radical leanings, but on the evidence of this, his first book, which was published in 1885, the plan obviously backfired. It is right around this time that Engels met Karl Marx, who read his book with great interest. *The Conditions of the Working Class in England* is often cited as a foundational text of their mutual project.

these people live in horrible conditions, that they're poor, exploited and so on, so its "heart is in the right place," right? But its tone is so egregious from the perspective of the present. It's so totally transparent in its biases... The signs of class difference are so transparent that it's actually shocking.

JP   Yeah, but I think that we're sort of outside of that. I think that this Marxist model doesn't really work with what's going on right now anymore.

JT   I don't know...

JP   ...I mean, you can still sort of use it, historically.

JT   I don't know. But, to some extent, I think there's still something useful about that way of thinking, that sort of troubled utopianism. Especially at the outset, where you have this sort of analysis that occurs, really, at the point of emergence of industrialism, and all these new urban centers, and urbanism as such, is a new phenomenon. And so you get a chance to hear from those people who are encountering it as new and different, as an unusual state of affairs—everything that we now take for granted. On that level, I think it always has a value.

JP   Meaning that...?

JT   There's a certain kind of alienated distance articulated there. That's the thing that really surprised me about Engels' book. I would have never expected that tone.

JP   Oh, really? Is it much more kind of body-conscious?

JT   Absolutely. It just goes on and on with descriptions of, you know, these filthy living conditions. The man was appalled and, at the same time, fascinated by it all. And I think that you're absolutely right: it's a new problem, this notion that you have to live together with those you exploit. Engels makes the point that this new industrial proletariat is just a bunch of displaced farmers. And so, you know, here's these people that were used to living in wide open spaces, with cattle, with pigs, and so on, and now suddenly they're here, all crammed-in together, and now they've got their pigs in the basement, or they're building these ramshackle lean-to pens or pigsties that spill out onto the street, and the animals are shitting all over the pavement, and that's a huge problem, you know? Because, as a boss, you have to walk through these same streets on your way to work, and you have to dodge all the garbage, all the smells and everything—amazing! It turns out that Engels lived a kind of double life in Manchester.

JP Wow, so he was a kind of a part-time intellectual, part-time businessman.

JT Right. A little bit like you in that sense, but maybe in reverse.

6

DIGITAL MEMORY
PRESENCE
ART WORLD INSIDERS AND OUTSIDERS
HETEROGENEITY
THE IMMIGRANT
MARXISM

Los Angeles
November 21, 2002

This conversation, conducted just under a month after the previous one, carries over some of its themes—above all, communism, which we return to near the end. No doubt, the frequent mention of Marx in these pages has to do with the fact that both of us had grown up in families that had fled Soviet-satellite states. Jorge had spent his earliest years in Castro's Cuba, relocating to Chicago with his parents and older brother in 1968, at the age of six. I was born in 1962—the same year as Jorge—in West Germany, "on the other side of the wall," to parents who had escaped Czechoslovakia in 1948, shortly after the Soviet tanks had rolled in. The experience of childhood in what might be described as ideologically overdetermined households can sometimes breed a deep-seated suspicion of ideology, whether communist or anti-communist, that is no less entrenched. Certainly, some of that can be made out here. Yet it should also be noted that, right around this time, Jorge was turning his attention to his most ambitious house-that-is-also-a-sculpture to date, an extensive compound structure in the Yucatán jungle that would come to be named *Tecoh*. The brief of this project, as initially formulated by its patrons, was philanthropic in regard to this economically disadvantaged region. As might be expected, this redemptive plan met with some resistance from the artist. Here we can see that the "egalitarian aspiration" that Jorge had claimed for himself early on in this book is aligned with a strict refusal to perform "good works" in any sense that could be considered socially instrumental.

JT   What were we just talking about? Oh, yeah, the function of computers on memory: how they expand our limited memory, how they give us a near infinite memory, which could help us to become more selective, maybe, in terms of what we remember. But then also, in the sheer surplus of information and stuff that it makes available, how that makes selectivity almost impossible. And the result is that we might be becoming more forgetful in fact.

JP   You don't have to remember anything with the computer; you just have remember how to get to stuff, how to access it. Memory is now something that needs to be there for other reasons, maybe poetic reasons.

JT   Memory of the older sort played a crucial part in conditioning a certain form of reception that could be termed, again, developmental, or evolutionary, or whatever. There is a lot of work out there that I think is responding to these new conditions of memory by not positioning itself in any kind of continuum, by claiming some new kind of autonomy, one that's related to the older kind, but is, at the same time, fundamentally different. As an earlier model, I'd say that Charlie Ray's work is after this kind of autonomy. Like, it's all there. You don't need a text, you don't need a line of reasoning, you don't need to pay attention to what he did before or what he did after—you don't need any of these things to "get it." The survey at MOCA (*Charles Ray*, November 15, 1998–March 14, 1999, Museum of Contemporary Art, Los Angeles), for instance, did nothing to expand my understanding of his practice. These works are made to be received one at a time.

JP   That's the ideally successful work of art: it has to manifest some kind of humanistic presence. The car has a life, you know, just like I do, just like the birds in the trees; sculpture has to have that too, in order to be sculpture. It's essentialist bullshit. Not to keep harping on Marx, but this stuff's so old-fashioned compared to the work of sociologists from even a hundred years ago. It's pathetic that the art world has taken up that problem, and it has been disengaged and fetishized and rarefied to the point where it can still continue to be valuable. I don't understand it.

JT   It's one of those things we'll never get over, I think.

JP   What's there not to get over?

JT We continue talking about modernism because it's something that's inculcated, by now, within our own desires and fears…

JP Do you know anybody who really believes that the world is going to get better? I don't know any artist who can really believe in this modern motionism anymore. Very early on, for me, it became clear that interesting works of art are about speculation. They're not about certainty, or that kind of control that idealism promises to fulfill.

JT I totally agree with you.

JP That's just the state of things. I think it's interesting; I think it's exciting. Works of art are things that connect to a world as well as a market, that allow you to sort of operate and take interest in things. And certain people have this facility to make things spin in a certain way and other people don't. It's a very big, complicated machine, and you have to be pretty fucking smart to be able to play.

JT Well, you know, it is an art *world*, right?

JP The art world is a handful of galleries who all meet in Basel, and now they all want to meet in Miami. Basically, it's all these people that allow themselves to sleep in every day.

JT That's one part of it. The other part is clearly that of the artists.

JP The artists are people that belong to that same group; museum directors are people that belong to that group; curators are people who belong to that group.

JT Sure. In a general sense, yeah. At the same time, I think they all speak somewhat different languages. They're not at all united.

JP But I think they're all ideologically positioned in a similar way.

JT I would say that the main area of contention occurs across the line of, let's say, this belief that artworks should operate efficiently, successfully, without friction, versus what you argue is the need for a problematic within artworks. I mean, even Charlie Ray wants you to look for a long time; he wants to ask questions; he's not after the "quick read."

JP   I think works are only successful when they're problematic.

JT   I think so too. But I don't think that a lot of the people that you just mentioned—those in the more "professional" positions of the art world—would agree that a work is successful if it's problematic. I think they'd have a hard time reconciling the problematic with this notion of success.

JP   I think that what we're talking about this afternoon, and what we're trying to sort of pick away and look at and split the hairs of, is the basic assumptions that a lot of people carry around about art. A lot of things that I learned in school are kind of worthless. And what's startling to me and interesting to me is that there's less and less of a difference between what was considered progressive and what this notion of the progressive once tried to defeat. Conceptual art is becoming more and more conservative. Michael Asher gets closer and closer to John McLaughlin the older he gets, you know? He was probably a student of his.

JT   But it's also there that, to some extent, you see that position on the problem—a resistance to craft, to the fetish, to all those things—being elaborated perhaps for the first time. Of course, there's Duchamp...

JP   I think that Duchamp, to a certain degree, was playing. I don't think Michael Asher is. I think that Michael Asher is someone who still has this very American way of making sure that the audience understands that there is something very serious going on in his work. And that seriousness kind of serves to sell the craft, because, really, this is just another version of craft. On the one hand, it's progressive: he chose to title things almost tautologically, to tell you exactly what the work's made of. But the problem with tautology is that it's already set and that the only reason that we use it is imperative. As a result, it's supposed to empty out the gesture, but in reality, it does the opposite. It's one of the quickest ways to reach a form of legitimacy. This idea that the farming out of labor, the fabricator, started with people like Michael Asher, I would say that's a compliment to him. But it has to be a good fabricator, a good carpenter. There's always that restriction: it has to be a good, quality carpenter. This idea that work of art is so progressive that there has to be a kind of defensive field in its didactics in order for it to be read as real...

JT   Hmm. Did you ever read the stuff Art & Language put out?

JP   A little bit, yeah.

JT   It's good, very well written, a lot of it. They're obviously arguing for a somewhat different version of Conceptualism.

JP   It's a little bit more interesting.

JT   It's much more anti-positivistic, for one thing. One point that they articulate really clearly is that, for them—and obviously they're saying this because they've moved on to a whole other sort of work—Conceptual art, like all avant-gardism, is really something that can only happen in an artist's youth, that it is the expression of these artists at a particular point in time.[17] All of the "leading lights" of Conceptualism developed their practices into these increasingly reified, rigid types of positions, but what there was initially did prize a kind of unskilled gesture—or, at least, prized things coming more directly from the world.

JP   I never think it's about the unskilled; it's about saying, you know, "I found it very interesting to go look at the plastic store. There was a much richer visual field there than I found in my studio."

JT   That's an insight that you actually worked with. You did that show at the MCA in Chicago that included a display of plastics, or glues, or whatever.

JP   Yeah, certainly. I don't discern between what's interesting here or there. I mean, everything can become an object in an exhibition—even the exhibition itself.

17   This point is articulated in a text from 1995 titled "We Aimed to be Amateurs" by Ian Burn of Art & Language. In it, he argues that Conceptual art "was practiced—and certainly animated—by relatively young people." At least, early on, "in its culturally radical, relatively untransformed form, [Conceptual art] is more or less *essentially* the work of people who saw themselves as in process. That is to say, people with a high degree of mobility, low security (and a relatively low perceived need for security), high discursivity, amenability to situatedness, possessed of a relatively meager economic base; fairly active in their efforts to extricate themselves from unwanted structurally-ordered determinations, and so on." Ian Burn, "We Aimed to Be Amateurs," in *Conceptual Art: A Critical Anthology*, eds. Alexander Alberro and Blake Stimson (Cambridge, MA: MIT Press, 1999), 443.

JT Right. But, to some extent, I'm saying that some of those positions that you're articulating, those were elaborated within Conceptualism and, no doubt, there were a number of different Conceptualisms, and then those became something still more different.

JP My problem is that Conceptualism would never abandon its connection to the necessity of a shtick, which is connected to style. The conceptual was uncategorizable until it developed a shtick and then you had a name for it. If you had to really inquire, then it may have been interesting … But it became a mode of identifying oneself with artistic presence more than anything else, and that's kind of pathetic …

JT … Because it's done in bad faith.

JP It's just not interesting. There's no reason to see it again; there's no reason to see that motion. There's no reason to sort of develop that motion any further when it's clear that it's exhausted. Just because an artist is interested in something, that doesn't mean much. But for the kind of Conceptual art I'm talking about, that means everything. In regard to the problem that I'm pointing to, that's a really important part of how somebody is taken seriously. It's how artists are taught how to project seriousness within their field of interest. So they travel, they go places, and they read; they start to dress a certain way and there's a whole kind of personal affectation that can then be used to read legitimacy into someone's interest, or something like that, which I've always found ridiculous. What is interesting to me is that, one moment, I can share my interest with you, and then turn around and enter a place where I don't even know how to be interested. The idea that somebody could be surrounded by these different experiences can be accommodated; it can be seen to have a *visual* sort of presence. You can show the thing, you can talk about it, you can show a picture of it—you know what I mean? And most art is about the opposite: it's an extreme and reductive kind of proposition.

JT But apart from, say, the blunt fact of heterogeneity, or the attempt to manifest a constant movement between one thing and another, can you talk about this any more specifically? Or is your work unspecific in its nature?

JP   Well, it is unspecific in its nature because it's not about legitimacy.

JT   **But when you look back at your own production over time, I mean, there must be certain lines of development that become more compelling to you than others.**

JP   Sure, but that's exactly what they are; they're not pluses or minuses or anything like that. I'm not about to make the jump and say, "This is the good one," just because it's interesting. And I'm fully aware of, and constantly in the motion of, returning to that same thing the next day and still being *uninterested* in it. Because, this notion of interest, it's unreliable. I wish it wasn't, but it's just the way it is.

JT   **When you talk about Warhol, it's because there's a similar kind of movement in his work, right?[18]**

JP   I think he understood.

JT   **Do you think it has something to do with his initial sort of estrangement from this culture that he's operating in? The immigrant aspect? I mean, that certainly does condition a different relationship to capital, commodities, the "glitz," right?**

JP   What being an immigrant does, when I've given it some thought, is give you a kind of presence within the world that's discursive by default, because you're always trading languages to understand. You know what mean? When I was speaking to Cesar Reyes this afternoon, I didn't know if we should be speaking English or speaking Spanish.[19] It's always this kind of trading off, not necessarily because it's a fair trade, but because you exhaust a vocabulary and revert back to another. And I think you look at the world that way as an immigrant because you're always trying to make sense of something other than those two cultural systems.

JT   **In being in-between systems you tend to lose a sense of focus, right?**

18   Pardo had recently spoken on Andy Warhol as part of the "Artists on Artists Lecture Series" at the Dia Center in Chelsea on September 5, 2002.

19   At this point, Pardo was still at work on Cesar and Mimma Reyes' house in Puerto Rico.

JP That's not the most interesting part of it, at the end of the day.

JT But you're holding these two positions in some kind of suspension, or dialogue.

JP You're fully conscious of these two modes as constructions.

JT OK?

JP So, if you're totally conscious of that fact, then there's nothing essential about any of it. As a result, you end up thinking about the world in a much more conditional, much more provisional way. It's like the same fucking thing could mean something totally different in Spanish than it does in English. That's a big deal.

JT Also, coming from what you might call a dominated culture, there is also this weird reversal that happens when you suddenly find yourself existing in this whole other imperial culture of winners, basically. Right?

JP Absolutely.

JT Because, on that level, you could say that Latin America and Eastern Europe, Cuba and Czechoslovakia—my parents' homeland—are similar. They have both been dominated for a long time, and therefore are also partly dysfunctional cultures.

JP This idea of the immigrant is important to a certain degree, but I don't think that it's totally formative—it's just an aspect of the work. I think that anybody that's relatively well-trained in discursive practices has to read things, has to look at them with that kind of analytical logic. Being an immigrant just makes you a little smarter, if you think about it.

JT That, to some extent, is also why Marx believes in the proletariat: it's because they have been dominated that they gain a particular perspective on power which the dominators don't have, and which the middle class has least of all.

JP Well, I would argue with Marx that the middle class has the most power because they are able to sublimate the most. Sublimation is what we're talking about.

JT   How so?

JP   Because the middle class is educated to point where they understand that people are lying to them. You'll see, we're going to go to the Yucatán, where the poverty rate is relatively high, though it is a functional poverty.[20] The educational system is not the best and Marxist emancipatory class cultures are always going to be clouded by a lack of academic infrastructure. Unlike the U.S., many people describe slavery in Mexico, particularly in the Yucatan, existing into the twenties. Most people don't have the kind of reflexivity that Marx was talking about; it's just not there. That reflexivity is a discursive condition that is completely specialized. It's only in the middle class. Somebody wrote an interesting article—it was in the *New Yorker* or something—claiming that the reason Castro was able to win wasn't so much because of the underclass; it was because of the middle class.

JT   Yeah, this is what all revolutionary leaders understood after a certain point, that revolutions are fought by the working class but won by the middle class. At the same time, that doesn't necessarily negate this question of insight. Because this insight that we're talking about is sometimes a very materialistic one; it's an insight into these very base formulations...

JP   It's a question of how do you legitimize unsanctioned languages? That's what knowledge is. You know, somebody lives in the jungle and they know every fucking bird that's going to kill them. It doesn't mean anything in America, but it means everything to

20 We are discussing an upcoming visit to the Yucatán, where Pardo had begun work on his largest project to date. This came about as the result of a commission by the former CEO of Banamex, Robert Hernández, and his wife, Claudia Madrazo, to somehow revitalize the site of a ruined hacienda that they had purchased about an hour's drive outside the city of Mérida. Originally an agave farm that later became a factory for the processing of henequen fibers, it was transformed by the artist into a sprawling compound of semi-discrete buildings, including a main house, a large kitchen pavilion, three guesthouses, and twelve *palapas*, all appointed with every amenity to luxuriously accommodate up to twenty-five guests at a time. The mandate initially proposed by its funders is that this place would operate as a kind of think tank for visiting students, scholars, members of philanthropic societies and the business world, etc., to mull over the fate of the region. Pardo, however, was always more interested in its function as a kind of inhabitable abstraction, a perceptual device. Work on *Tecoh*, as it came to be named, was completed around 2012.

someone in Brazil somewhere. It's a valid thing. The problem with Marx was he didn't understand that those things have to be instrumentalized, particularized, in order for any kind of difference to happen within a social space. I mean, people had to believe in Marxism; they couldn't actually partake in Marxism, and that's the problem. Anytime you sort of ask someone to take a leap of faith, they're going to be fucking robbed.

JT   All of these grand teleologies, they all have that sort of messianic underpinning, and they all demand a leap of faith. Because it's a total system, right? And to enter a total system you have to totally renounce the one that you came in with.

JP   Anybody that's not clueless is going to feel like they're being scammed. We were initially talking about audiences, right?

JT   Yeah, but to some extent, I was simply talking about memory and concentration ... as something that can be sustained over time versus broken up into these discrete instances, which is increasingly all I think that artworks are asked to do: to concentrate an instance.

JP   Yeah, I think that's what they should be asked to do.

JT   Do you think so?

JP   Yeah. I think that actually they're asked to do something much more supernatural or something, but at the same time, all work is asked to be present as an instance. It's like I was saying earlier: I'm initiated, I'm educated, but I'll assume that everyone loves different kinds of blues and oranges, and that those things can bring pleasure to the eyes or whatever. But then those things are also asked to kind of have depth, and that depth is what allows a different kind of class to set it up as a kind of deep kind of currency. And I'm suggesting that it should only be an instance, but not an instance that's considered deficient because of its lack of depth, but an instance that's interesting and prescient because it's connected to the present and that has a very particular type of memory inscribed in it. That's what I'm interested in.

JT Yeah, I like that idea because you can't discount the fact that history becomes inscribed in the present.

JP I think that good works of art talk about what's going on at the moment, and they do that in an insightful way. You can't really do that when you're playing both sides of the fence.

7

THE EIGHTIES AND NINETIES IN L.A.

DURATION AND THEATRICALITY

THE EPIPHANY

ARBITRARINESS

SCULPTURE AND PHOTOGRAPHY

PRICE POINTS

Los Angeles
January 29, 2003

It is only in retrospect, while supplying the footnotes to this book, that I have come to realize just how many projects Jorge was juggling at this time. While the *Tecoh* project was in development, work on the aforementioned Reyes House in Puerto Rico and the guesthouses in Denmark was still ongoing, and this is not to mention any of the smaller commissions that were by now flooding into the studio, or the solo exhibitions that had to be regularly mounted at the artist's various galleries in L.A., New York, Berlin, Tokyo, and London. In addition to this, there was the series of "activations" that Jorge had been invited to perform in the mixed capacity of an artist, curator, exhibition designer, and event coordinator at the Dia Art Foundation, in Chelsea. It is to these latter efforts—which followed his attention-grabbing incursion into Dia's ground-floor space in 2000—that this conversation is mostly devoted. The word "motion" repeatedly comes up here. "It's more interesting to not necessarily make important what the subject of a motion is," says Jorge, "but to find out what's important through the motion itself." And, of course, this way of working requires one to keep moving.

JT   There was a boom of some sort, though, in L.A. art the nineties.[21]

21 Before the recorder was turned on, we were discussing Pardo's participation in the ambitious group exhibition *Public Offerings*, which was curated by Paul Schimmel and held at MOCA, Los Angeles, between April 1 and July 29, 2001. This show featured the works of an international cadre of young artists that had made their mark on the art world almost immediately after graduating from art school. To an extent, Schimmel had attempted to reconstitute these artist's first ventures into the commercial gallery space within the space of the museum—hence the analogy to the public offering of a fledgling company on the stock exchange. The artists were grouped by city, and described between them the reconfiguration of the network of art capitals that took place the nineties. Included among these were Berlin, London, Tokyo, New York, and L.A. Pardo was assigned

JP In the end, the eighties were much bigger than the nineties. It seems to me that the whole European element never quite crossed over in the nineties, and that's the only thing that really made it, the L.A. situation, in the eighties. Its whole potential got very much wrapped up in Europe. It doesn't do anything to show anything here that isn't doing something bigger somewhere else.

JT But the one thing that certainly did happen during the nineties was that L.A. art was being exported at a rate that hadn't been seen before—that it was gaining a great deal of attention elsewhere.

JP But not that much in relation to what's going on there.

JT But I think you're right in regard to the fact that no connection was cemented, or that L.A. galleries never took the initiative to establish lasting bridges to Europe and the rest of the world, right? Los Angeles galleries just stayed put, in a way.

JP They stayed put … China Art Objects tries, but their internal structure is so open that they just sit.[22] I don't really have a market in L.A. like I have in other parts of the world.

JT Is that right?

JP I never sold anything over twenty thousand bucks. People who collect art in L.A. don't have a feel for it. That they'll spend, like, a

to the latter city, alongside Diana Thater and Jason Rhoades. Not caught on tape was a comment, spoken by him, to the effect that L.A. constituted the weakest link in this chain.

22 This gallery opened in January 1999 on the touristic Chung King Road in L.A.'s Chinatown. Its location was originally a souvenir shop, from which the gallery kept only the signage and name: China Art Objects. It was founded by a group of friends with a shared a background at the Art Center College of Design in Pasadena; these included Giovanni Intra and Steve Hanson, both close friends of Pardo. Certainly, this association to an already established artist—Pardo, and also Pae White, who was largely responsible for designing the interior space—was instrumental to the gallery's success. It played a key role in fostering the Chinatown art scene in those years, which, by the start of the aughts, had emerged as a youthful alternative to the somewhat more established scene in West L.A. The frustration that can be made out in Pardo's tone, however, might imply that there is an expiration date on the allure of scrappy non-professionalism.

hundred thousand on a Richter piece, or maybe a Doug Aitken or something like that ... I don't know what to think about that work other than it's touching a very sensitive kind of a commercial vein.

JT   **I think the work that does well connects very directly with Hollywood, the film industry. Generally it's non-Conceptual ...**

JP   ... Generally it's a kind of flaccid sculpture, like Lawrence Carroll. These people are always around; they come from the illustration world, and at some point, they make a leap, or somebody realizes that there's some sort of currency there. The art world has always had those kinds of people: the Starn twins, Lawrence Gipe ... there's always been a market for that kind of thing. Ultimately, record covers are much more interesting venues for it than the exhibition. I think these are people who don't have the ability to understand what the terms are for an exhibition. You know, like, what's at stake in exhibitions, or why does it make sense to show this in a gallery.

JT   **Too true. Well, on that subject, I was interested to learn from Lynn Cooke that you are planning to show your boat in the Dia space, possibly?[23] Which turns that space into something akin to what you did in Chicago and in London, doesn't it?**

JP   I think they're just going to store it.

JT   **Anyway, aren't you employing a similar strategy at Dia, where there is, as you say, a folding and unfolding of events in the gallery spaces. It's not a static installation; it's something that changes over time.[24]**

23   Lynne Cooke was the curator of the Dia Art Foundation between 1991 and 2008. Pardo has had a long-standing relation with Cooke and this institution. His exhibition at its former location in Chelsea, New York, laconically titled *Project*, ran from September 13, 2000 to June 17, 2001. Rather than mount a show of discrete works in gallery, the artist had opted to redesign Dia's front lobby and furnish it with a spacious bookstore in back. These street level spaces were integrated by way of a continuous flooring of colorful ceramic tiles that also crept up and encased the columns, bathing the once austere venue in a somewhat riotous atmosphere that Robert Irwin famously compared at the time to "a cheap Mexican restaurant." Pardo's sailboat was never shown there, but other found objects were—notably, several objects and pieces of furniture by Alvar Aalto and a full-scale clay model of a 1994 Volkswagen Beetle. Thereafter, Pardo would periodically reactivate the space as an exhibition platform for his own works as well as those of friends in a manner that might be compared to the MCA Chicago initiative.

JP There's kind of an irregularity installed in the duration of the exhibition. I think that's one of the problems with art in general: it doesn't really deal with duration.

JT **There is, as you say, a durational element, and therefore also a theatrical element, in a way, right?**

JP Theater doesn't deal with duration. Duration, for me, it's like the space where you blend the theatrical with the real, you know what I mean? There's a big distinction between the theater and theatricality. Theater, it's narrative; it has its own narrative; it has its own structure for the way it marks time. Beginning, middle, end. First act, the lights go on, then there's a monologue, and the audience comes out at the end.

JT **Of course, there's all sorts of ways within theater to mess with that, and to break with those expectations and structures.**

JP Yeah, but the frame is always the polemic, you know? Like, the "living theater" concept is interesting not because there might be a gallery involved or anything like that, but because you always have the potential for some Midwesterner to show up to see somebody go poop on stage, that kind of stuff.[25]

JT **There's something about this idea of theatricality that could call on an active spectator, one that decides when to come, when to leave, how much time to spend in front of something—all these**

24 Following the displays devoted to Alvar Aalto and the Volkswagen Beetle, a 1969 sound piece by the Italian sculptor Gilberto Zorio titled *Microfoni* was exhibited in the third iteration of Pardo's *Project* at Dia (Jorge Pardo and Gilberto Zorio, *Reverb*, September 19, 2001–June 16, 2002). A selection of small works by Gerhard Richter was entered into the fourth iteration (Jorge Pardo and Gerhard Richter: *Refraction*, Sept 5, 2002–June 15, 2003). Finally, Pardo presented a full-scale plywood structure constructed from a kit that he designed to serve a variety of functions "ranging from a house in the tropics to a movie theatre in an urban park," as noted in the Dia brochure (Jorge Pardo, *Prototype*, September 17, 2003–January 11, 2004).

25 The Living Theatre is an experimental theater company founded in 1947 by Julian Beck and Judith Malina. It was originally based in New York and was responsible for exposing American audiences to the work of Bertolt Brecht, among others. There is an evident confluence between the work of The Living Theatre and what would come to be known as performance art.

very pointed sorts of decisions, right? These aren't in the theater because, there, to some extent, the timeframe is set. To suddenly leave, you break with it, whereas in the gallery there's really no breaking with anything. It's all up to you.

JP Duration is also something, the way I understand it, that's always being co-opted by absorption, which is the kind of event that happens in front of a picture in a particular space. In theater, absorption never really is an issue.

JT Really, in theater?

JP In theater, because the context is one where everybody's watching each other. You're trying to keep up with the lines, but you're not thinking of the theater as something that has depth, you're think-ing of the theater as something different—it's flat. Take this glass (he holds up the glass he's been drinking from) in the theater this is something that is much bigger than a normal glass. It's theatri-cally bigger, but then, again, it's also flatter; you can't walk around it, for one thing. In all these spaces, you have to locate these kinds of differences, and these are very interesting ways of looking at exhibitions.

JT You're talking about props? The idea of art as a prop?

JP Yeah, but I'm also talking about how absurd it is to even think that this argument has a susceptibility to theater. Which is kind of what's wrong with Michael Fried: he basically didn't understand how significant it is to be in front of a picture versus in front of a stage.[26] He didn't understand it to the degree that it's really not possible to talk about artworks as an artist's props. They're not props. Objects have duration, they have the capacity to have someone consider them over time. Duration is duration. Theatrical devices have the same potential as any object in a room; it's just that their rate of absorption and consumption is faster. They don't have the capacity to narrate, they don't have the capacity to make motions, to docu-ment. They're not connected to documentary at all.

26 This, again, relates to Michael Fried's "Art and Objecthood," which is where the terms "theatricality" and "absorption" are employed in opposi-tion to each other.

JT   Right, I got it. But let's take your work at the MCA in Chicago, or again at Dia: it seems to me that when you shift these objects around in this space that we generally understand as a static space—a space that one moves through, but where the space itself and everything in it generally remains still—clearly it's challenging our expectations and perceptions of…

JP   …It's saying a bunch of things at the same time. What it begins with, maybe, is the question of whether there's a reason for the artwork to be here for more than just a couple of days. Or whether there's a reason for this particular work of art to be considered a certain way. What does that mean? How long does it take people to sort it out? Dia's motives are kind of from the nineteenth century, you know? They're classical; they're more academic.

JT   They are. There's always some kind of attention paid to the placement of particular works in the larger arc of the artist's career. Attention gets paid to historical context, to provenance, and these types of issues that are related to classical museology, right?

JP   Yeah.

JT   So, let's say in your Dia installation, to what extent are you working with or against those types of expectations? First, by locating your work downstairs, in the lobby and in the bookstore, and second, by changing it over time. You change it in much the same way, maybe, that a bookstore's own displays are changed on a regular basis, or every time something new comes in.

JP   Basically, I'm arguing for a mode of presentation that seeks a kind of efficiency that's like other things in the world. I mean, the best an artwork can do is arrest your attention and produce reflexivity, you know, make you look at something again, and maybe think differently about something you kind of thought you knew, which is what ultimately what I think a work of art does. And that's the difference between a work of art and a piece of theater.

JT   Ultimately it deals with the familiar, not the strange or exceptional, right?

JP Not necessarily. But, again, its mandate is to interrogate and to manipulate some notion of duration. To put the question of the work within the problematic of what it's like to be in this awkward place—you know, between an exhibition and waiting for something to happen.

JT What's that other place, then? Could you define it more clearly? If the exhibition represents one side of this problematic, then what's on the other side?

JP It's the sort of space where you just sit around and wait for something to happen. In other words, it's the spiritual element, or something like that. It's fucked up; it's like going to church.

JT Is that some kind of sublime, spectacular experience you're talking about?

JP The spectacular... You know, there are many, many instances where people talk about being arrested by a work of art, or a work of music. Like Brian Wilson [of the Beach Boys], there's that story he tells about that song by The Ronettes, "Be My Baby." He talks about hearing this song while driving his car and how he had to pull over because he knew that that was incredible, that he had witnessed something spectacular. He says the same about the Beatles...

JT Something about this has to do with the fact that you recognize it, the work or the song. It's not something odd that's coming from some unfamiliar place, but something that you recognize. In his case, in particular, it's always something that one could have done or should be doing, or...

JP ...Yeah, it's always understood in terms of something that was missed. In other words, it's kind of a narcissistic thing.

JT Someone got there first.

JP It's a narcissistic projection.

JT It's an interesting example because you can say, well, that's because he's a musician listening to music, but to what extent is all work received in that way? I mean, the moment you become someone who goes to galleries with any kind of regularity, you are, to some extent, aspiring to that place of production, right?

JP   But not everybody is aspiring to *that* place of production. I know I'm not. I like to think that I make works of art that one can turn away from and then return to, and not necessarily idealize, you know? Like, I don't really make works of art that help me struggle, through their qualities or values or anything like that. If I make a painting and it doesn't quite work, or it's kind of different, or maybe it's ugly or something, it's like, my impulse is to look at it, stick it up on the wall, because I know that it's about a series of relationships that may come into play in the future. I'm making things for myself to see. I'm not putting myself in a position like Brian Wilson, who prefers to remain tormented. What drives the self in his case is a kind of tormented process; that's what motors that stuff. If something big is not happening, it's horrible: he feels like shit.

JT   I'm just saying that, to some extent, you could look at that as a kind of exaggerated or over-determined version of what happens on a subtler level in our general relations with cultural objects. Because anyone who is a big reader of books, let's say, at least coddles the notion that they could be a writer or that they are becoming a writer. Likewise, people that go to galleries a lot leave a space open—whether or not they're going to act on it doesn't matter—but a space opens up for a potential producer. And yet, that space, I think, is necessarily conflicted. For someone like Brian Wilson, who is neurotic, that conflict is momentous; for other people, it's just a subtle nagging sense, perhaps.

JP   Yeah, but I think it's idealized, that neurosis is really idealized in this field. In a lot of places, it's one of the components that confers a kind of legitimization, and it tends to become absolutely central. Laura Owens, whose work I think is great, is someone who really believes in that. Like, for her, the things that move the work are these adventures, these kinds of epiphanies. I mean, there are a lot of ways to make work. Why does that particular mode of production have to be centralized as the bulwark of the artist's legitimacy?

JT   I see what you're saying.

JP And that's why you work: you can condition your abilities so that you can have as many of these different epiphanies as possible. At the crux of what I do and the way that I work is an opposition to that. Because I think that...I don't want to feel that way, period. It's not that it's good or bad; it's just not an interesting way to negotiate the world for me. I think it's more interesting to have a much more diffused sense of experience, you know what I mean? A lot more can happen.

JT Right. It's something like what [Gaston] Bachelard, using the language of psychoanalysis, talks about as a form of absolute sublimation, which is a necessary precondition for the poetic image to come into view.[27]

JP It's all bullshit! It's all bullshit!

JT But what he's saying is that one can sort of forget about one's self and sort of move past neurosis thanks to these poetic images, which, incidentally, don't have to be momentous, which can be perfectly mundane.

JP But I don't think he leaves the problem behind.

JT No, because he uses that language...

JP ...What's at stake in that kind of problematic is finding a way to exit the dynamic, but not necessarily its effect. Banality is sometimes only at the service of a dynamic of superiority, and that's pretty fucked up. That's fascism, you know? Most infrastructures of the twentieth century were invented by fascists. That wasn't done by the hippies; that was done by people who actually *believed* and had *vision*. I'm questioning how productive something like that really is.

27 "The phenomenological situation with regard to psychoanalytical investigation will perhaps be more precisely stated if, in connection with poetic images, we are able to isolate a sphere of *pure sublimation*; of a sublimation which sublimates nothing, which is relieved of the burden of passion, and freed from the pressure of desire." Gaston Bachelard, *The Poetics of Space*, trans. Maria Jolas (Boston: Beacon Press, 1994), xxix.

JT   Can you just talk very frankly about how shifting the objects around over time, say, within the Dia installation, functions to dispel or …

JP   … It deprioritizes their objectness. It basically levels the hierarchy between one thing and another. It makes it so that one just comes out in the other, and hopefully it kind of doubles it. There's no room for an epiphany in any of this stuff because everything is presented in the same way, you know? Like, the floor is there; the bookstore is there. The bookstore is just as effective a frame as the floor is, or a boat or a house or a Richter show is … It's one of the things you need: you need to have that kind of an attitude in order to move through things. The reason that I've sort of resisted this other problem, this other mode of working, is that it doesn't really make room for analysis.

JT   OK, which is related to the next question I was going to ask you: clearly this way of shifting things around cannot be completely arbitrary, right? There's a limit to its arbitrariness.

JP   The notion of the arbitrary is always susceptible to duration, to how long something is done for. At a certain point, there's a kind of pattern evolving, you know? The notion of the arbitrary obviously has to do with thought because things will start to resemble one another even when they don't in actuality. So, there's an anticipation, there's a structured way of viewing that's produced by these gestures I deploy. I mean, I hope, and I *think* that if I continue to be involved in just these motley presentations of things, then maybe a different kind of mediation can happen. In the way you consider a house next to a shoe next to a table next to a chair next to the land, for instance, that you start to understand that a lot of the things that we take for granted—how things are good or how things are bad, or what's an interesting work of art—are pretty much arbitrary. It's not a terrible thing that it's arbitrary; that's just not productive, nothing interesting happens when you think that way. Because in order for it not to be arbitrary, it has to have consequence, and I'd argue that there has to be a rupture in your ability to process that kind of thought. And I think that's the whole problem in a nutshell: this rupture is not based on an epiphany. And anyway an epiphany is just kind of a flashback of what you're looking at. As a rule, epiphanies take things away from you. I'm doing the opposite: I want to bring them forward, or something like that.

JT Right. But, again, in terms of forwarding a certain form of arbitrariness, clearly the parameters of every project are going to shift and you're going to address something specific about these objects in this specific space.

JP The arbitrary is never forwarded; it's produced. There's a difference...

JT OK, let me just ask you, then, would you say that arbitrariness is always the same?

JP No.

JT No. So what is it that varies from one kind of arbitrariness to the next?

JP Just the motion among parts; that's it. You do one show, and then you do another and another and another. It's all within an arbitrary mode, and although I don't think you can really control the quality of the arbitrary, it does sort of shift in some way, and you start to develop a kind of language...

JT And to some extent, I would say, when you start speaking in those terms, what you are doing, ultimately, is assigning some kind of meaning to things, however tenuously.

JP I don't think you have to. I think the way you talk about things is everything. The way you talk about things is your whole motivation, but without necessarily pointing to some ulterior discourse, you know what mean? I don't think people talk very interestingly. I think language is something that coincides with production; it's not necessarily outside of it, nor wholly inside. It's just... you need it. The way people think about the discursive in the work of art is ridiculous: it's clearly still a burden.

JT If you're saying that they don't intersect, that theory and practice might be running parallel or something, then I agree. Because there's no place where you can make the one fully cover or account for the other, and yet they generate each other in some way.

JP Yeah. They depend on one another, but at the same time, they do different things...

JT I'm still curious, though, in the way you talk about arbitrariness, I can't get away from the idea that it might be something that is very easy to produce.

JP Yeah, but try doing it in an interesting way.

JT OK, then, that's my question: what makes an interesting arbitrariness? And furthermore, how does this idea of arbitrariness develop over time to become more interesting?

JP I don't think you can handle it that way, theoretically.

JT When you're talking about developing a language of arbitrariness, I think it's pointed in that direction.

JP Yeah, but those motions don't necessarily have to be thought of that way. When I talk about the arbitrary, I'm talking about being ambiguous or underdetermined, something like that. I think it's interesting because it allows you to be in the work as a viewer, a spectator, and as a producer all at the same time. That's the only reason to do something like that, because you're managing to avoid idealizing the work of art… You can have kind of a fragmented relationship to what it is. You can be just as confused as a producer as you would be as a viewer, you know what I mean? Like, how do you do that? You want to sort of fragment the operation that produces points of view within the work.

JT OK. That, to me, seems like something that you do quite consistently, and, in fact, a large amount of your output is directed towards doing that in different ways as you go from one context to another.

JP I think that's important.

JT You always have certain objects that can stand in for point of view, let's say, more than other objects. There's typically a kind of object that can represent looking or that can represent consciousness in some superficial or abstract way. Even a lamp, a signature object for you, could be thought of in this way. By placing that object into a larger assemblage of objects, you are already fracturing perception, perspective, POV.

Fig. 8 *Untitled* (Reyes House, Puerto Rico), 2004.

Fig. 9 *Untitled* (Guesthouse for Krabbesholm Højskole), 2001.

Fig. 10 *Project*, 2000. Installation view, Dia Center for the Arts, New York.

Fig. 11 Table with routed-out cameras, 1988.

Fig. 12 *Pinhole Camera*, 1987.

Fig. 13 *Pinhole Cameras*, 2001. Installation view, Friedrich Petzel Gallery, New York.

JP   They're more like optical devices. It's not anything different than somebody like [Jean-Luc] Godard was trying to do when he was making those early films. It's about a certain kind of loading up of imagery without any concern for how it affects the hierarchy. Everything that happens, happens at the same time; it's all happening simultaneously, over and over. The idea of simultaneity is the motor for an interesting poetics, I think. It makes for a space where you can get lost, and then you can go back in, and there's these fragments that you can sort of put together into sorts of wholes—see how it's set up? I'm interested in making a work of art that doesn't resist your ability to consume it, but makes it enormously difficult to totalize it. Because it's not static; it's actually changing all the time. Like, I'm trying to get each show to do something different. Apart from just being interesting, this is really important, I think, because it allows you to stay away from a shtick. And then it's like going to a trade fair or something like that. You always know that something new is coming, something different, something … you go because it moves. The way things move is through differentiation, you know? I try not to repeat motions.

JT   Right. That's maybe why it remains productive to think of you as an L.A. artist: because there's something in that way of thinking that reflects the layout of the city. There's no representative view; there's no single place that offers you any kind of overarching perspective. To know L.A., you really have to move across it.

JP   You have to move. In order just to be in L.A., you have to move. That's the only kind of presence that it really has.

JT   But then again, I think that what you do as an artist is, to some extent, to structure a movement through things, to structure that passage or trajectory, and you do it differently from one show to another. There's a perception of something developing or building, over time …

JP   Yeah. I mean, it's pretty simple. Maybe I'm interested in something and then something else, I don't know … It's more interesting to not necessarily make important what the subject of a motion is, but to find out what's important through the motion itself. This sort of sidesteps the theoretical positioning, you know, so that the theoretical doesn't necessarily enter into its process of production.

Instead, it becomes a framework that you need to look at it, or something like that.

JT I think that certain things must happen when you're in the process of structuring these shows. Like, you have one show and you're changing it over time, and there's certain lines of development and certain kinds of narratives that begin to emerge, and these will suggest further opportunities, like, where to go next. You can make certain analogies between what was there and what is there, right? And the same holds for the audience: I think people won't be able to help making an analogy between the clay Volkswagen at Dia (fig. 10) and, say, the boat.

JP What do you think that analogy would be?

JT What do I think? I'm more curious to hear what you …

JP … I don't know what it's going to be; I just want to put a boat or a car in a show, you know what I mean? I'm always surprised at how even a simple gesture like that always has the ability to frame itself. That's not to say that I have no idea; I can load it up with meaning. I can say that these are both transportation devices, they move. One's affiliated with a certain kind of American idealism, and the other, with a different idealism. You've got two classes: you've got a car representing a certain class and a boat representing another. Why say it? Everybody knows it.

JT The Volkswagen is the ultimate model of a kind of populist transportation.

JP Exactly, it's the hippie car.

JT Right, but born from the Nazi car.

JP If you start to think about things that way, that's an interesting sort of polarity. If I want to pick a color, I'd have that in mind. What would be an interesting color in relationship to that kind of a conflicted equation? I mean, that's how you move through the motions of the work. These things are not ideas, because there's always room for, I don't know … There's always room for something else to happen.

JT The thing I appreciate so much in your work is that you make it very clear just how something is thought through. It's not about ideas, as you say, but there's a process of thinking that becomes evident. It's that you're thinking on your feet, that you're facing one decision after another, and you're leaving this trail. I can see the build-up of those decisions and, to some extent, I think the most successful works are the ones that are structured almost as a chain of thoughts.

JP I would agree.

JT So, as you say, there's no point at which there's a grand epiphany, or where any of these thoughts become totalized as one thought. Instead, what you do see is this process of analogy—that is, the sequence of analogies that makes the thoughts possible. You know, this thing plus that thing equals a color or shape...

JP I like that, that the work is driven by analogy and analysis, and not necessarily by a visionary impulse. From very early on, I've always used the word "speculative"; that's very much congruent with your thinking. I'm interested in the speculative potential of these juxta-positions, and I'm fully aware that setting these things into motion can make them bigger than I can think of, or different... That some-thing will come back to me.

JT That you can surprise yourself.

JP Not surprise, but that you can give yourself something to think about. It's not like playing tennis by yourself or something like that; it's like making a robot that looks back at you. It's different, and I think that's really important.

JT To some extent, all artists want their works to look back at them or to speak back to them, but, I think, with what we're talking about...

JP ...That's at the forefront. It's what's structurally significant about the work for me. With most artists what drives the work is more a formal expertise or something like that. They want these shaped paintings, let's say, to give off a kind of fuzzy effect in an inten-sified way, and that's about it. That's what they're after: they rarify, rarify, rarify to the point where they become experts in this rarefied gesture and its result. Most artists make works so that they can be left alone.

JT   They're the only person in the world that can do this one thing.

JP   Yeah. It's a lot like rubbing up close to something, and not in the best way. There's fictions and myths that support it. When I make architecture for an exhibition, for instance, I'm fully aware of the potential for a certain amount of volatility within the given discourse that I'm engaging, and I want to know what that is. I want to know because I think most architects are idiots. You know, I'm trying to understand what is the shape of the aesthetic in houses or buildings? What's significant about making a door a certain way or another? Why make things that resemble something else? But that's just the first question; that's what structures the beginning of the work.

JT   That's the prerequisite for any sort of analogy to take shape: there has to be a resemblance of some sort at the beginning of it, right?

JP   You're saying that all works of art are produced through this kind of displacement: an artist makes the work, and, in the process, they make a viewer, and the viewer sort of looks back at the artist through the work, right? That's very different than saying, OK, let's start with that; let's do that from the beginning. There's a double, this thing's already got a ghost—what now? That's the question; that's the problematic.

JT   This thing being what?

JP   A consciousness that comes about through resemblance, by imitating a certain aesthetic, by using a certain material—a material that's used in other things, say—and by always remaining conscious of the fact that things are used in a very straightforward way, so that there can be equivalent analogies. If I use a piece of board, I'd like you to think about a tree, or about Japanese woodworking, or about ecological issues—anything, really. But I don't want to cut it short in some sort of ideological way; I don't want you to figure those kinds of interpretations ideologically. I like them to happen in a more ambiguous way. I think that the ambiguous and the arbitrary are things that help you to enter this kind of this space.

JT   Right. What you're talking about, basically, is play, and play can only occur within the space of certain parameters. These are very simple and arbitrarily set, but they still have to be considered, acknowledged; they're the rules, right? You have to have rules in order to play ...

JP   It always presupposes somebody else: the dummy, you know, some reduction of yourself. It's complicated.

JT   I think, in play, in games, the rules function to diffuse the ego in some way; that's why they are very simple and arbitrary. There's a different sort of decision-making in play that's not based on ego, or that you don't have to feel entirely responsible for. Yet it remains an exercise of some sort: you're exercising your mind and your body. More importantly, you're interacting, right?

The conversation resumes after a break.

JT   So, what we're discussing is movement, seeing while moving, making connections on the fly, but we're also discussing the course of this movement and how it's structured or composed. I wonder what you think of Ruscha's early works in this regard—those books *Twenty-Six Gasoline Stations* and *The Sunset Strip*, for instance?

JP   To photograph all the cars on Sunset Boulevard is obviously ridiculous. In relation to the thinking of everybody else around taking pictures of cars, or taking pictures of one car and thinking about it compositionally ... it completely flies in the face of that kind of realism. It's basically saying that motion, movement, these different things being in different places, is what makes the work.

JT   I thought that the reason it's apropos is that it amounts to a portrait of L.A. This representative street is less a place than a surface on which signs are posted—it supports all these billboards and signage, right? And the only way to picture this thing—not only this street, but L.A. in general—is to move through it. So this becomes a segment, a part, where our awareness of the whole of L.A. is somehow heightened. But then what's also interesting is that he takes all his photographs and lines them up, end to end, and makes this accordion booklet out of them so that our experience and our view of this thing can fold in on itself and fold back out. You can look at the whole thing or you can look at it part by part. I think that this format is highly meaningful and, in fact, that's where the work's whole meaning lies: in the way that the experience folds in and out.

JP   In and out, that's a sort of precondition…

JT   …And also, what's interesting about this object is that it exists in between almost every available medium. It's a book, but it's made of photographs, and it's also like a strip of film—a road movie. So, it's about a kind of "mediumicity," but, at the same time, as you say, it's such a ridiculously simple work: it's about a guy taking photographs out of the window of his car. And then, of course, you have to take the car into account, which is something that you tend to do in your work as well. Again, I'm thinking about how you'll often have what I take to be these displaced or abstracted stand-ins for point of view, and how they're typically tethered to some sort of vehicle, right in the middle of your shows.

JP   I don't think about them that strategically. I mean, they're interesting; cars, I'm interested in them. Believe it or not, though, the Volkswagen at Dia was Lynn's idea.

JT   Really?

JP   To a certain degree: she found it. So she said, "Are you interested in this object? Do you want to do something with it?" And I go, "maybe I'll just stick it in this spot." She's interesting; I mean, she's somebody I feel is really in tune with what's going on in the work.

JT   I can't help but think that the car is a camera. Even though it's made of solid clay, it can be seen as a mobile camera obscura, just like the boat was and might again be. It's literally a room that moves through space, a room that creates a particular point of view, and also a kind of externalized consciousness, in that sense.

JP   Yeah, you're actually one of the first people to have expressed that opinion.

JT   But hasn't that always been the function of these things? Right from the start, it seems, you were rethinking the sculptural object from a photographic perspective. There was that table with the routed-out cameras that you installed at Bliss (fig. 11), for instance.[28]

JP   I got a lot of attention with that. But I did an earlier body of work, which was shown at the Art Center student gallery, of things that could photograph themselves.

JT   Oh yes, the coffee cup that photographs itself in a bathroom mirror (fig. 12) ...

JP   The cup was just one example; I also made an owl camera. It was made from one of those owl statues that people put in their gardens to protect their plants. I remember that Tom Solomon wanted to show the resulting photographs, the images that these things took of themselves.[29] I didn't want to show them. I thought they would produce a kind of artificial context, a context that I couldn't understand being transposed. But it made sense initially: I felt that I wanted to make work, when I was out of school, just to see what would happen. In the end, it was good not to show them, because you can always show them later ...

JT   ... Didn't you, in fact, go back to making pinhole camera pictures?

JP   I did another show just to reinvestigate it.[30] (fig. 13) The point there was to make a book. So, the show had about fifty photographs, costing ten or twelve dollars each, and these were compiled in a book that cost fifty thousand dollars. Of course, it didn't do so well. I liked the show; I thought it worked, because what I was trying to

28 Bliss was an artist-run gallery opened in 1987 by Pardo and his colleagues from Art Center College of Design, Kenneth Riddle and Gayle Barklie, in the garage of the house they shared on 825 North Michigan Avenue in Pasadena. Pardo mounted his first public one-person exhibition there in early 1988. It featured a table into which he had routed several cavities that could function as rudimentary cameras, so that, with the assistance of a mirror, it could photograph itself.

29 In 1988, Thomas Solomon, the son of New York art world luminaries Holly and Horace Solomon, opened his own gallery in a two-car garage in Hollywood, which he ran until 1991, thereafter moving to a more conventional gallery space on Fairfax Avenue. Jorge Pardo's first solo show at the Garage, as it was called, took place in 1990. There, the artist exhibited a collection of tools and everyday objects—a router, a set of wrenches, a ladder, a sheet of plywood, a length of two-by-four, etc.—either painstakingly remade by hand or somehow altered.

do was to sort of rearrange the dilemma of reproduction, to move it around a little bit. I wanted to make people feel that their mind was a camera and that, if they used it in that way, then they could create the book for themselves, instead of just buying it. In a way, the book had to have this absurdly high price to put off the public, the collectors—but also to motivate them.

JT   Also, this is not a representative object for you, right? It doesn't necessarily look like "a Pardo."

JP   I like those things. I like those projects a lot because I think that they are like gaps or stumbling blocks in regard to people's expectations.

JT   Would you say that it's a disappointment?

JP   Yeah, for certain people it is. A lot of people want a painting, even if it's coming out of a computer; they want something "pure," something they *really* can't afford … Most people don't understand what is interesting in the work that I make. It's completely relational. In order for it to happen, there needs to be a kind of space to run that has nothing to do with paintings or sculptures, you know? It's motion. What I do now when I work is, I generally ask a collector for five or ten thousand up-front, which is non-refundable, and then I'm going to come up with something for you.

JT   That sounds like a lot.

JP   Richard Serra asks for fifty thousand, and a lot of collectors think it's an insult.

JT   Because it's the collector's prerogative to choose things; they're experts at choosing.

30 This show, titled *Pinhole Cameras*, was presented at Petzel gallery in New York between October 10 and November 12, 2001. Quoting the gallery press release: "The exhibition will be comprised of fifteen mono-chromatic, geometric forms housing 'pinhole cameras.' Each sculpture will take a black and white photograph of another, and the resulting photographs will be compiled into a book."

JP   Once you enter that space, you immediately get objectified. Buy something that's already around, or tell me what it was, and I'll make it for you, but I don't want to get involved in a flat discursive enterprise with people who don't understand what the fuck I'm doing—at least, not on spec. It's a problem.

JT   That's an important aspect of the work, I think. We've talked about it: that way you have of stepping on toes, right? Because all of these various parts of the contract between the artist and public that you want to manipulate, all of these functions and all of these spaces, are already taken up. You've got your curators, you've got your dealers, you've got your critics, you've got the buyers…

JP   … These are all producers.

JT   They are, and they exercise their own private field of expertise, and yet your project often exceeds its bounds and strays into those fields…

JP   It mobilizes the limits. It makes apparent and clear what the bottom line is. Like, a dealer shouldn't be making art; a collector shouldn't be making work—it's a bad idea. If you want to collect, you have to collect in a certain way: you become *familiar*. To think that anyone who's got ten million bucks can put together a really good collection is stupid. You just end up with a bunch of John Currins and Elizabeth Peytons and maybe a couple of Jorge Pardos, and this means nothing. To actually make something worthwhile takes a totally different attitude. I think the work does step on toes; it makes the person who bought it aware of a kind of limit. It's an uncomfortable notion. A lot of things about it make you uncomfortable, and the work's not working unless that's clear.

8

THE RESEARCH ARTIST

HISTORIES OF CONCEPTUALISM

THE FUNCTION OF POP SONGS

Los Angeles
March 3, 2003

That our conversations regularly returned to the topic of pop music was largely at my urging. Throughout this time, I had been writing a string of articles on the relation between art and popular music for a number of local and international periodicals, including *Artforum*, *Frieze*, *Flash Art*, *Artext*, and *X-TRA*. Also, I was planning a series of discussions on the subject (with such figures as Kevin Hanley, Dave Muller, Frances Stark, and Mayo Thompson) that were slated to begin in just a few months at the newly opened Mountain Bar in Jorge's Chinatown studio. I was then taken with the thought that so many members of my generation had been inducted into art through music, not only as listeners, but also by navigating the whole semiotic complex of the album cover, lyric sheet, promotional film, newspaper interview, bedroom poster, etc. Sam Durant, the artist we spend some time discussing here, could be seen as exemplary in this regard, yet he is not taken up in a favorable light. The harshly critical tone that we indulge in is more a response to the work's naively enthusiastic reception than it is any kind of statement on the work's intrinsic quality, which we had not really even begun to consider. Ultimately, this conversation circles around the relation of art to research. Durant here serves as a kind of foil, a straw-dog antithesis to Pardo's own approach to subject matter.

JP His [Sam Durant's] work seems to be dependent on very clear political topicality.[31]

31 We are talking about Sam Durant because his survey exhibition was up at the time at MOCA (October 13, 2002–February 9, 2003). On view were works dealing mainly with the fraught legacy of modernism from the sixties onward, notably a series of vandalized models of Case Study Houses that had attracted a great deal of attention in the press. Also included were works referencing Isamu Noguchi, Rosalind Krauss, Robert Smithson, the Rolling Stones, and Kurt Cobain.

JT   The work makes all these references. It touches all the bases, all of the existing points of this given constellation of thought.

JP   Yeah. It's like playing the daddy, or something like that.

JT   My feeling about it is that if you're going to make those particular connections between art and rock music, say, I think you have to begin by stepping back and citing them as given, already determined, or even clichéd. You can't bring them up as if the connections were new and provocative in their own right, which they aren't. The job of making those connections has already been done.

JP   Right, right. But it's provocative within the art world. It's supposed to be radically discordant in an aesthetic chapel. Mike [Kelley] was doing something like that.

JT   Do you think it's still gaining some mileage out of being disruptive?

JP   Absolutely. Have you read the catalog?

JT   No.

JP   This catalogue has a very serious tone. To be precise, he's even described as if he's kind of reclaiming this history, or how going back to those sources, how that is a progressive way of dealing with this history, of redeeming it.

JT   Hmm.

JP   In other words, there's a believer at the end of the whole thing, right?

JT   As I understand it, what he does, to some extent, is to say that while this history of art—this history that we all know—is unfolding, these other things are also happening all around it, and there's a partly secret history of interconnections taking place there. There's a kind of assertion that this can be recovered and rendered viable in the present day. But the only thing that's new about those connections, I'd suggest, is that they're being made now, and they're being made somewhat casually, right?

JP Yeah, basically there's a softer tone to it. But I think that if you had a good art history teacher, you can't really talk about Richard Serra without thinking about the Beatles or the Rolling Stones... How can you do that?

JT Exactly. So what I'm trying to see is where does the provocation reside? This is basically Pop art, an established category, which has to do with a conflation of high and low poles of the culture.

JP It doesn't mean anything to make these connections. Why don't these connections mean anything anymore is the question. Here things maybe get a little more interesting.

JT If you're writing as a historian, say, you're going to have to find something that hasn't already been found, maybe something new. You're actually going to have to uncover some overlooked piece of information, which is not really what's happening here.

JP Well, he does these kinds of base working-class jokes; he adds this other thing...

JT Yes. So this is Pop art plus Conceptual art, or rather an undoing of Conceptual art by Pop art—that's exactly what we're talking about. I think that all of this hinges on a standard assumption about Conceptualism, a wrong assumption that is pervasive...

JP ...That it's an exclusive, elitist...

JT ...That it's the epitome of the "high" in "high art," right?

JP Right, which is not it at all.

JT But, again, I think that might be an interesting proposition if you were to deal with it on the level of cliché, recognizing that this is a pervasive reading of Conceptual art that is wrong, a misreading. And maybe this has something to do with the failing of Conceptual art itself, to be so misread. And to bring that into the question might be interesting.

JP That's taking art school maybe a little too seriously.

JT I'd argue that there is a lot of work out there that takes it both too seriously and not seriously enough. To go all the way with these propositions would mean becoming really involved with this material, really booking-up, you know, and not stopping at this generalized understanding of the thing. To begin with, it is interesting that Conceptual art tends to be so misread, that there is a pervasive concept of it as elitist when, in fact, it sought initially to undermine that position. This might lend a whole other reading to these attempts to juxtapose it with, you know, these images of working-class slovenliness...

JP It's a cliché: taking a working-class scatology and applying it to the highfalutin', right? No matter how these operations work, at the end you've got the product—the "ha ha." These things, they're not revelations; they're very straightforward. It takes me thirty seconds to put them together.

JT Here's the thing: I think there are basically two ways you can operate as a historian or a critical theorist. One of them is that you discover something new or make a new connection, and the other is that you take an old connection, but you use it as a springboard for new thought, new speculation. As an artist who might relate to the second position, let's say, you've got a tremendous amount of leeway. You don't have to follow the rules of good scholarship, you know. That's ostensibly the advantage of being an artist and not a historian or a critic: you can really take off with your research.

JP You've got to offer an interesting way to read this history, or to think about it as art.

JT There's an alternate understanding of Conceptualism that's been gaining ground, and it makes a lot of sense to me. So, on the one hand, you've got these artists who sought to undermine the existing processes of commodification and they sought to do that through this sort of lower-class opposition to the elitism of art. But this other understanding is that Conceptualism was looking forward to a new information market, where information itself becomes a commodity. It was seeking out ways of packaging information and, on that level, it was looking to the future.

JP It's just looking forward.

JT But that's an interesting rereading, I think. But it would mean really grappling with the original context.

JP Who are the people responsible for the first reading? Shitty painters, right?

JT Umm, yeah…

JP … The only people who talk about Conceptual art as something elitist are people who want to go back to looking at pictures.

JT And the opposite is true as well. That's the point I was making in regard to Baldessari: I wrote a while back that the paintings he torched weren't exactly "hot" to begin with, you know?[32] Conceptual artists wanted to stop looking at pictures and start looking at the world, drawing connections between already existing things, "composing" them in that way.

JP Baldessari… I think that the older he gets, the more conservative he becomes and the more his practice is grounded in traditional issues of space. And not necessarily social space, either; we're talking about something purely formal.

JT The *purely* formal, absolutely. I think he is increasingly interested in again mapping out that flat space of the picture plane, right?

JP So, what's the main connection? Let's connect the dots.

JT So, I think that, more recently, a lot of attention is being given to people like Seth Siegelaub as being among the main agents of Conceptual art, those people who faced this dilemma in a very practical way: how do you sell information?[33] In so doing, they're thinking ahead. I think that's interesting.

32 To demonstrate his commitment to Conceptualism and to its logic of dematerialization, John Baldessari sent the entirety of his painterly oeuvre up in flames. This drastic move, which laid waste over one hundred works, resulted in one final object: a modest funerary urn with a plaque bearing his name and the dates "May 1953" (his college graduation) and "March 1966" (his turn to Conceptual art). The event that yielded the *Cremation Project*, as it came to be titled, occurred on July 24, 1970. I wrote about this work in the essay "Baldessari's Urn: On Nineties Art in LA," in *Artext* 71 (November 2000): 42–51.

JP I do too. And I think it does come from this position of marginality. For the first time, you have a different class bringing this informational currency to the table, you know? And what the fuck is formalism going to do about it? Zero.

JT **You make a good point.**

JP It's not about going against it; it's not a polemical thing; it's an irrelevance. It makes total sense: I mean, these are suburbanite kids. The GI bill dies, and people who didn't like the Ivy League didn't get a chance to change their opinions, you know what I mean? These are Catholics who've got a lot of frustration with the world. A lot of working-class people from California, surfer kids, people who at no other time in history would be allowed anywhere near these kinds of cultural places, you know? And then you've got the right wing, people who still want to be able think about Barnett Newman as somebody who's progressive. These positions are incommensurable. There's no reason to even try to manage some sort of relation between them.

JT **Exactly, there's a complexity there that it would be really interesting to try to, let's say, map out. But, again, it would require a certain kind of rigor, to actually look at the specifics of the situation we're talking about. You can't be reductive with this stuff unless you make it clear from the start that you are only dealing with a clichéd version of the facts.**

JP A lot of current work just doesn't move with complexity; it only moves because there's this other operation, which is actually quite pathetic, and it has to do with the belief that the level of complexity of a pop song, let's say, is equivalent to a speculative

33 Seth Siegelaub (1941–2013) was a dealer, collector, curator, and researcher mainly known for his early advocacy of Conceptual art. In addition to mounting some of the first shows of the artists assembled under that banner—the most notable being those that contained no physical artworks, but rather dematerialized information, such as *The Xeroxbook* in 1968—he was also responsible for rethinking the sale and resale of art as a form of intellectual property with his "Artist's Reserved Rights Transfer and Sale Agreement" document of 1971. The crucial role played by Siegelaub in aligning Conceptual art with the still-emerging economics of immaterial goods is analyzed in Alexander Alberro's *Conceptual Art and the Politics of Publicity* (Cambridge, MA: MIT Press, 2003), which I was reading at the time.

complexity. I think it's really interesting how you describe pop as a language of systems and not a language of ideas. So much recent art uses these pop structures as idealistic structures as opposed to positioning structures. You talk about a relational system that moves: a song on the radio gets you to the record album, the album cover gets you to the poster, you know, and that helps you to get laid in the back of your car. It's all this stuff, and you can't think about any of it in terms of being direct.

JT   No, and you can't even think about it as having a specific meaning at any given stage…

JP   You know, I don't understand it when people say, "That's a really great pop song!" That doesn't mean anything, because pop music, to me, is a lifestyle medium. It's about expediency; it's about going in your car; it's about daydreaming about being somewhere else. It's not about making a great piece of work. It doesn't need that kind of validation; that only serves to shut it down. It stops the circuitry of motions that makes the thing interesting.

JT   Well, you've got these two systems that do literally intersect at various points. For instance, I just read the other day that the Rolling Stones wrote some of their lyrics using William Burroughs' cut-up method, and of course Burroughs is very clear about the fact that this method originates in the visual arts. So, the band is using this Surrealist or Dadaist mode of composition, and that's a concrete link between these two contexts—one among many, many others. It's interesting stuff to read or write about, but where do you go from there? Is it enough to simply point this out, or is it just the first step?

JP   You've got to look deeply inside a medium, and not necessarily be worried about identification. Something else you wanted to talk about?

9

CHANGING PATTERNS
OF RECEPTION

CONSCIOUSNESS-RAISING

SENSATION

FOLK CULTURE
AND KITSCH

THE HANDMADE VERSUS
THE READYMADE

Los Angeles
Mid-2003

The dating once again becomes blurry; the best I can say is that this meeting occurred in the middle of 2003. Here, we mostly stick to the subject of craft. It struck me on first encountering Jorge's work that it relates to Conceptual art and yet is manifestly, if not idiosyncratically, made. That is, it is not just made "well" in the generic sense that Jorge previously attributed to Michael Asher and his "good carpenter." I had for some time wanted to hear him put the particularity of his aesthetic into words, and am rather persistent on this point. However, it quickly becomes clear that Jorge will not take the bait; along the way, uncharacteristically, he even admits to feeling "stumped." Whether this is a sensitive issue for him or, rather, one of no interest is hard to gauge. Nevertheless, even if only by way of deflection, a number of provocative arguments are voiced—for instance, "craft is always an afterthought."

JT   What I want to talk about today—and we have touched on this before, I know, but only in passing—is changing patterns of reception. I'm thinking about the different ways art is received these days and the different ways that artists try to accommodate this—let's say, accommodate a shorter attention span on the part of the public, or what have you. The connect-the-dots, evolutionary model of thinking about art is becoming impossible. This is certainly not something we were taught at school.

JP   Yeah, that's a manifold question. We're both returning to the apex of Conceptual art, and to people who've been trained by Michael Asher, either directly or indirectly. When I say this it's because I think that, methodologically speaking, there's really not a big difference between Stephen Prina, who I studied with, and Michael Asher, who you studied with, in terms of their sort of "sartorial" style. But one of the things that I took away with me as a student was that Conceptual art is kind of wrong, that its perception of the world is uneducated, visually unsophisticated, a sort of vulgar Marxist proposition. The same impulses were evident in, like, the literacy debates. This came from the Eastern Bloc and the Third World countries in a way—these places where art was given an instrumental role in "schooling" a broadly illiterate public—that's the model for the social function of Conceptual art. It deluded itself into thinking that it actually could propagate enlightenment, and in order to do that, it had to kind of rethink the audience and, at the same time, not rethink it to the point that makes it impossible for there to be work. There's always been this tension, and that's the hypocrisy of it.

JT I'm thinking of the Conceptual artist, you know, "a stone in the road," stenciled words on the wall? Lawrence Weiner. Anyway, he gave a talk recently where he stressed his own working-class roots, and also then talked about the need to address a working-class audience, or to be, again, working with some notion of the proletariat in mind. Which is all the more perplexing when you get to Conceptual art because there's this very overt disconnect, in social terms, going on there.

JP It's a kind of an ideological implosion that happens in Conceptual art. There's an authenticity that it can no longer rely on; there's the idea of an audience whose consciousness doesn't need to be raised. And the reason that consciousness-raising is so important in Conceptual art is in the making of markets. It's true of Kosuth and even Asher, to a certain degree—because, even though Asher's always disassociated himself with the market, it remains for him a very necessary polarity. He's also in a position to do that; he's independently wealthy.

JT But for someone like Michael Asher, the function of the classroom and of teaching is actually intrinsic to his practice. I suppose that you can project that educational model, to some extent, onto the work, like in the way that it demands a highly focused attention over time. And, you know, this cannot be projected onto the market, which cycles through concepts and forms very quickly, right?

JP I guess what I'm trying to say is that I don't believe that.

JT No?

JP   No. I don't agree with *The Society of the Spectacle*, where Debord says that the only sort of non-spectacle, the only place where spectacle doesn't happen, is in the academy. And this argument is very much along the lines of what you're proposing.

JT   "The educational"—Debord actually uses that term, I think.[34]

JP   The academic, the academic. It's because there's a perception of a different kind of depth there that's equated with time. And it's literalized in Michael Asher's classes: I mean some of them go on for twenty hours. I'm much more somebody who sees the world like Warhol, or Walter Pater.[35]

JT   Ah, the one that's responsible for that famous quote: "All art aspires to the condition of music."[36]

JP   Yeah. It's not a question of intensities or depth; it's a question of sensation, you know what I mean? It's not important how deeply you know something, but it is important that you be open to as many things as possible.

JT   That's interesting. That concept also, in a sense, comes to light under Romanticism. Even the term "sensation," that it should be the central aim of art to somehow stimulate our sensations … A certain sort of learning takes place there, but it takes place through the body.

34   For instance, in a text from 1955, Debord mentions a proposal by the Belgian Surrealist Marcel Mariën to relocate "all the equestrian statues from all the cities in the world … in a single desert. This would offer to the passerby—the future belongs to them—the spectacle of an artificial cavalry charge, which could even be dedicated to the memory of the greatest massacrers [*sic*] of history, from Tamerlane to Ridgeway. Here we see reappear one of the main demands of this generation: educative value." Guy Debord, "Introduction to a Critique of Urban Geography," *Situationist International Anthology*, ed. Ken Knabb (Berkeley, CA: Bureau of Public Secrets, 1981), 7–8.

34   Walter Pater (1839–1894) was a British scholar who wrote mostly on literature and art. Not a name brought up often in contemporary discussion, this reference signals Pardo's very catholic taste in reading material.

36   Music is, for Pater, "the ideally consummate art … *All art constantly aspires toward the condition of music*. For while in all other kinds of art it is possible to distinguish the matter from the form, and the understanding can always make this distinction, yet it is the constant effort of art to obliterate it." Walter Pater, "The School of Giorgione," *Studies in the History of the Renaissance* (Oxford: Oxford University Press, 2010), 124.

JP It makes a burgher or somebody like that feel like they're connected to a kind of history.

JT Sensation, I think, asserts the primacy of the body, that you learn through the body.

JP You learn through experience.

JT So what you're saying, then, is that you don't see that concentration is a necessary part of this process? Concentration sustained over time?

JP People's acquisition of language is involuntary. I spent most of my time as a kid watching TV, and that gave me a certain kind of fluency in a certain kind of an image repertoire that I know is changing. When I got to college, it seemed absurd to me that there were these individuals like Michael Asher—you know, old-school style hippies—who were saying that this experience couldn't really be productive within the poetic field. And instead of the poetic, you were force-fed this idea of raising consciousness. And, you have to remember, I'm somebody who's coming from Cuba, from an exhausted ideological domain that's basically degenerated into a totalitarian state. But this is usually whipped up and given the spin treatment by these people. Take that big guy who runs the Whitney program, you know, Ronald Clark: it was a big deal for him to go to Cuba on vacation in the seventies. Or, say, Gabriel Orozco: it's very important for him to talk about how he's a recreational Marxist down there in Mexico City. The kind of Marxism that's deployed in the art world really has nothing to with the kind of repressive moralism that I experienced. I could never take that stuff seriously.

JT You know, it's still very much a badge of honor within art schools to say that you don't have a TV, or that you never watch TV. And then, for the ones who do admit to watching TV, it's always passed off as a sort of guilty pleasure.

JP I don't believe that anything that happens involuntarily is bad. That's puritanism.

JT You're right. I totally agree, and I think that this whole argument also comes out of Romanticism. It has to do with that point in time when folk culture starts to give way to kitsch, or when kitsch splits off from folk culture. Kitsch is characterized as a sort of cold, distanced, fetishistic form of folk culture, which is initially about experience. Folk culture is concerned with the literal kind of experience that Benjamin talks about.

JP   Technology makes that possible. The reason this stuff splits up is because you can have thousands of these little Eiffel towers that are made in a little machine. And then there's the notion that any kind of an object-value, of a cultural object-value, has to deal with a way to put that experience back into these things. Then there's a kind of real stake, a way to connect to these things that has to do with how they're made. I think that's really where it gets kind of fucked up. Someone like Pater or, to a lesser degree, someone like Oscar Wilde, will instead see these openings where there's an instrumentalization of kitsch, where kitsch becomes an instrument for the first time. Kitsch has become separate because it's no longer connected to the guilds; it's now connected to commerce. It's a representation of these market forces for the first time.

JT   And the other thing that happens when it becomes disconnected from these guild societies and joins the open market is that it loses its sense of a specific audience, and instead it has to imagine a generalized or generic audience. Or, at least, I would say that that's the argument that's leveled against it. That's why popular culture or mass culture is seen as being essentially cold whereas, let's say, folk culture is intimate and intense and ...

JP   ... It's real.

JT   Right. Because folk culture is precisely what Benjamin's figure of the storyteller disseminates.[37] He inscribes his specific experience

37   Walter Benjamin published his essay, "The Storyteller: Reflections on the Works of Nikolai Leskov" in 1936. This was an early stab, on his part, to distinguish between different modes of cultural dissemination, what later would be defined in terms of an "oral culture" versus a "culture of literacy" by bona fide media theorists like Marshall McLuhan. Benjamin cites the figure of the novelist as one who has broken the interpersonal chain of information exchange. "The birthplace of the novel is the individual in his isolation," he writes, "the individual who can no longer speak of his concerns in exemplary fashion, who himself lacks counsel and can give none." Both kitsch and autonomous art emerge from this break. Walter Benjamin, *Selected Writings, Volume 3: 1935–1938* (Cambridge, MA: Belknap Press), 2006, 146.

into the story and then passes it on to a specific listener. And that whole contract, in all its intimacy and intensity, becomes diffused under these new conditions of spectacle and kitsch. Which, again, is not necessarily to say that it becomes obsolete, or that there's no longer anything that you can do with it...It's interesting, I just recently reread that short text by Oscar Wilde— I think he includes it as an introduction to *The Picture of Dorian Gray*, it's just three or four pages of his theory on art—and it's all about this love of the superficial, right? It's about the frivolous and, obviously, in this regard, about sensation. Dorian Gray is all about that stuff; he basically gluts himself on superficial or sensational culture.

JP He's somebody that, for the first time, maybe, is a kind of a non-essential being.

JT To an extent, his essence, if you want, becomes split as a result of representation.

JP His presence becomes contingent, discursive, representational. It becomes sort of impossible, you know? Because it's a phantasm, an image—literally, a picture that's talking back to him.

JT You mentioned that the way something is made is maybe not, or maybe should not be, a principal concern. But in regard to gaining a grasp on your own work, the thing that I always fall back on is that the early pieces were made very differently than later ones. Maybe this just has to do with the arc of your career.

JP They are made in different ways. The earliest works that I made when I was in school were really expedient forms.

JT But, let's say, you made them by yourself, and...

JP ...It doesn't matter who made them. What matters is that I've never had a sentimental relationship to production; I've always had a kind of problematic relation to it. Even when I made things by hand or whatever, it was always very clear that I was really calling attention to how stupid it is to value the individual, this essentialized individual, in any reading of the work.

JT I would say that expediency becomes readable, a salient part of the work, because you're not a master craftsman, possibly?

JP But some things I made were intended to never read that way either. I tried to develop a rather sophisticated relationship to visuality and craft. Like, with the two-by-fours, or a piece of plywood (fig. 14): there's not much space in an object like that for to me to do anything.[38] You know, if I were going to carve or whittle something by hand, then it turns into a very sentimentalized sort of thing or position. But the two-by-four got made in the same way that anything gets made: it's like, two cuts on a table saw. You know what I mean?

JT So there's very little room to mess things up or to inscribe a gesture or signature of any sort.

JP There's just very few motions that are required to make that work. And there are other works that required many motions. And then there are works where I didn't do anything at all; somebody else did it. I was hoping that people would read that there was a kind of discursivity that was being deployed. I wanted to get you to start thinking about questions like, How does one read investment within a motion inside a gesture inside an artistic production?

JT Let me ask you, then, if that question stays constant over the years?

JP It's not produced; it's a given. And it became a given because I feel it's something that's lacking in art.

JT But isn't that a concept or a condition that you yourself have elaborated?

JP It's a given ... Take the pallet (fig. 14): if it doesn't get made that straightforward way, then it will not be able to exist in the present, to a certain degree, as anything other than a fetish. And I've always tried to avoid fetishism because I think it's uninteresting— it's like caricature. It can only be seen as a naughty thing, right?

38 This refers back to Pardo's first solo exhibition at Thomas Solomon's Garage gallery in 1990, see note 29.

I'm not interested in that, in anything that's going to place me into some sort of puritanical position or something like that.

JT Still, I'm wondering if that idea is one that has been elaborated over time. And how?

JP It's elaborated over time because whenever you try to of enter a work in this kind of Romantic or sentimental way, you're always going to be deferred to these kinds of absurdities, and then you're not being selective any longer. I was always interested in the question of how do you frame choice in works of art? How do you make works that talk about how absurd it is to actually sit there in front of something and actually make a choice about what to do. Because, in reality, there's nothing that hasn't been treated much more interestingly than anything you might come up with. In a way, it's an attack on Duchamp in that, you know, I don't necessarily think that his project is all that valuable to us in the end. All it can sort of produce is a dichotomy. All it can produce is a kind of polarity; it's an either/or problem, you know? Where either it's art or it's not-art.

JT You think?

JP Yeah, absolutely.

JT I think there's much more to it than that. I think there's a homology that's formed when he brings all of these different sorts of items into the space of his practice. Again, it's in the way that it all comes together, piece by piece, over time. He starts making analogies that are formal as well as conceptual, and he begins to elaborate this universe that is highly sexualized and also reflexive, and ...

JP ... I think that that project's relation to figuration is what kills it. If he had tried other sorts of things, like amoebas or something like that, then maybe it would work. But he's talking about sentimentality. He's talking about a mechanical bride, a kind of synthetic desiring machine.

JT In the mid-teens, though, those were very compelling and relevant concepts he was putting out there, I'd say.

JP Yeah, but those concepts were already being discussed by sociologists at the end of the nineteenth century. From Weber to Marx, it had already been elaborated, what the problem was. In the end, this work is much more advanced than anything Duchamp did.

JT Well, you've got these philosophical, discursive practices which are obviously stationed in the realm of language and the idea, and then you have art, which really tries to deal with the thing. Duchamp, I think, elaborates a position between ideas and actual things at the same time as the object-world itself becomes discursive.

JP I don't think he's very convincing. I don't think anybody really understands at the beginning of the century that what artists, what interesting artists, are working with is this discursive motion. Like, the fact that we can no longer think through objects through production, through the work of the hand ... You have to deal with objects some other way. You have to deal with film, you have to deal with propaganda.

JT Which is something that he deals with very emphatically, film. You could say that all of his works from a certain point onward—say, *Nude Descending a Staircase*—are about film. How does film affect our perception of ourselves? Even the bicycle wheel, for example, bears an analogy to some kind of a filmic fascination device. I mean, who else, would you say, is onto this? Who's making important strides into that field at that time, according to you?

JP I think that you have some of the photographers from the Bauhaus, like Moholy-Nagy or basically anybody who understands the poetics of mechanization. Anybody who's trying to set up a poetic within a mechanism—that work is going to be interesting to me. The Futurists also, to a certain degree, but they're so stupid they don't really produce anything worthwhile. They're actually illustrators of the problem or something like that. And it's clear why fascism and Futurism merged, ultimately, because it's not enough: the problem is not digested, it's regurgitated ... It's aestheticized.

JT I recently played one of those Marinetti sound-poems—you know, *Parole in Libertà*—for my class. It was great. I have this very old recording, full of scratches, and the man sounds so utterly insane. And you can only imagine that those people actually were insane, and that the avant-gardes were these dysfunctional networks that were formed to maintain and protect their own delusions, to an extent.

JP   It's classic, it's just classic. The insane are only productive when they prevail under the auspices of the super-rich. Insanity is worthless to people who work; you kill these people, you get them out of the way. You figure out a way to have them take out your garbage. That's the mentality of class; anything other than that is a perversion. That's not to say that some interesting things can't happen, but ultimately ... Let's say, the reason Picasso's not interesting is because Picasso's world is not the world of anyone that actually desires those paintings. These worlds aren't really connected. We look at a Picasso because we can't stand the sight of ourselves.

JT   Picasso could be seen to follow a trajectory related to yours. He starts out with a somewhat conventional relation to his craft and then proceeds to break it down, to analyze its parts. But I'd still like you to describe your evolution from an earlier point to now. How does the idea develop, your relation to this craft concept, this sort of non-fetishistic, anti-idealistic concept of production?

JP   I don't know ... Nothing gets made without craft. But craft is sort of synonymous with control, and control is sort of synonymous with instrumentalizing. Because, basically, what artists do today is walk around the world and make points of view so that people can look at things that maybe resemble what they know as reality, or maybe they're models ... And craft has nothing to do with that. So, I'm thinking, "What would be an interesting definition of craft that would actually mean something to me?" I don't know.

JT   It sounds like you're trying to generate a more varied field of, maybe, intermediate gestures. So, there's an attempt to elaborate a non-fetishized, expedient, maybe even casual kind of craft. This does seem to be important for you in general—and I'm not saying you're aiming for consistency here.

JP   It's a kind of casual expediency, period. Craft is always an afterthought.

JT But the only way that that can be communicated is, again, by how the thing is made.

JP I'd like to think that there's a way to look at a work of art where the question of, "Was it made well?" or "Was it made poorly?" has no play. That's why I feel kind of stumped.

JT OK, I'd say that, even the position you're talking about, even that, can only be elaborated in the making of something a certain way. I don't want to talk about it in those terms, "well" or "poorly," but...

JP I think that, at times, there's a certain amount of visibility within human gestures. We were talking about cooking last night, and about how, right now, everybody has got open kitchens. Nowadays, it means a lot to be seen as you're entertaining, versus twenty years ago, say, when that had no social currency. But, in terms of this question of "Where am I in the work?" I always think that that's completely contingent on motions that I can't quite control. I've always found this sort of reading to be very problematic. A position like mine is one that tries to circumvent that, disallow that, make it possible for that kind of reading to not mean much.

JT How do you do that, then?

JP You do it by jumping around all the time: by making things that your mother makes, by making things that your dad makes, by making things that your dog makes, by making things that a robot makes, by making a painting that takes you two seconds to make, by making a painting that takes a two thousand dollar computer to make it in two seconds. You do it by movement. And the move is to make clear that... well, either you're going to be obsessed with it, or else you're going to realize that it's not going to help you. You're going to realize that the relationship that's implicit between what was done and where it's going, that it's somehow evading that problem.

JT That movement, again, I think, is something that can only be communicated over time. By someone who's been connecting the dots, to some extent...

JP ... To somebody who's reading the work as a project, which is something I think you do if you're interested. I mean, we live in a time where it's very easy for my nephews, let's say, to get on the computer and look at twenty-five projects of mine. They're all right there.

JT   And the interesting thing is that the computer, which disseminates your project, is also the thing that's responsible for the dispersion of your project, or every project...

10

SUBJECT-OBJECT RELATIONS
THE AURATIC
MEDIATION
THE HISTORICAL AND THE UNFINISHED

Los Angeles
October 24, 2012

As a general rule, I would have transcribed our last conversation before the one that follows. This meant that I often met Jorge eager to resume a topic that he may already have left far behind. Since the discussion is here again largely directed toward questions of craft, the handmade versus the machine-made, I can imagine that this might have been a source of annoyance to him. This is probably the most contentious and bristling encounter here. I am rightly taken to task for sentimentality for speaking of the "warmth" of a maker's touch. Yet, for me, the question remains open as to how exactly this artist manifests not only his position but also his person within his work. Even a "non-essential being," as Jorge put it the last time around, is not without a sensibility, and perhaps it is even more pronounced than that of an essential being. Although very little of this discussion about modes of production actually touches down on his work—it mostly taken up with critical theory—indirectly, by way of analogy, an aesthetic attitude is clearly expressed. "The problematic of the unfinished," says Jorge, "is everything that I'm interested in." This is the perspective of an artist who is always thinking ahead to his next project, whereas for me it is more important to connect the dots, which means thinking backward.

JT   We never really filled this part out, and it's something that's really important to me in understanding what you're up to. I don't know if you still agree with this, but there's something in your work that has to do with looking at one medium through the perspective of another. In particular, that is, looking at sculpture through the perspective of photography, or through the perspective of information technology. This begins with the coffee cup that photographs itself in a bathroom mirror and then that table that's been routed out and outfitted with cameras, and it goes all the way through to the use of the boat-as-camera in that show at the MCA in Chicago, and maybe also the car-as-camera at Dia. There's always some kind of technical model of reflexivity that's being put into the material space of sculpture and architecture.

JP Yeah, you've pretty much summed up my concerns. Once I became involved with architecture, the question became: what do notions of *expansiveness* mean? How does somebody actually deal with space in terms of leaving a place behind and entering the space of one's head? What happens when you're not *in front* of the artwork any longer? How do associations actually stay connected to these experiences and how can you maximize them? In other words, I was never interested in making architecture in the conventional sense, but what I was interested in was this: if you actually go into a place, and if you decide to make this wall green as opposed to white or something like that, there's a certain kind of motion that gets stopped. You've made a reflexive space inside of it, and once that's in there, then you can kind of bring other things into it. What can you put into it, what happens then? Or, more precisely, to get to your question, what happens when inherently reflexive mediums such as photography—but also sculpture, painting—are used in that way? They get kind of mixed up, muddled up in these quotidian kinds of frames. What are the differences between quotidian reflexivity versus aesthetic reflexivity? How do I stop? What makes me stop the work? That was always a question I was most interested in: how do works of art stop?

JT What is a table with a camera in it? Is it a table with some capacity to image itself, or imagine itself?

JP Yeah. It has the capacity to image its form; it has the capacity to be seen as something that can see; it has the capacity to kind of survey; it has the capacity to compose things. Basically, it's an anthropomorphic application of these kind of formalistic structures.

JT That's the kind of thing that becomes really interesting in light of this discussion about industrialism as the point at which a certain kind of ability to look back is taken out of the object. That's Benjamin's whole description of the industrial object—it no longer meets or reflects the gaze. Actually, he's talking about painting as much as he's talking about mass produced things.

JP   I would agree. I mean, with Benjamin, but also more generally, there must have been this assumption out there that the kinds of reflexive structures inherent in pictures somehow weren't getting at the kinds of experiences you were having out in the world. Pictures are like tools with which to consider qualities, values, whatever you want to call it, but they don't really work anymore. Because, at a certain point, people's desire, the intensity of their desire, is equivalent whether they're going into a store or viewing a complicated artwork. That's the fear, and I think there's a problem with it. I actually think Benjamin's theory is an oversimplification...

JT   ...He talks about the quality of the handmade thing as having a deep kind of reflexivity, which is different from surface reflection.

JP   He never gives up the auratic.

JT   No, and the auratic is described in specific terms as that which allows the object to somehow look back, no matter what it is, even a table or chair, because it's been infused with the existence of its maker.

JP   I don't believe in that at all. I mean, I was reading Benjamin at the time I was making the pinhole cameras in school—that's where that whole project comes from. So, I made a cup—and these things can never really see themselves; they always need a mirror—but I made it so that it could photograph itself. One of the pictures is of the cup reflected in a mirror in the men's room, and what happens during the exposure is there's these six guys that pee. It's going to take up six or seven minutes for the exposure to happen. So, on the one hand, that image is a kind of caricature of what Benjamin is talking about, and at the same time it's a debasement of what Benjamin is talking about. Because if the auratic is somehow in cahoots with the object-subject problematic...

JT   ...Which comes down to the gaze...

JP   ...Right, who's looking at it. So, the person who's looking, who's got the vantage, plays the subject; the person who's being looked at plays the object. I mean, all these kinds of questions ultimately end up being about these kinds of old-fashioned ideas about being human. What these pinhole pictures did is to make it possible to corrupt those kinds of questions. They said, "Yeah, that's interesting: this is the object, this is the subject, this is the camera, and it's all the same thing." But if you stop there, you're not looking at the most important part of the picture, which is that something strange happened: somebody peed. And then peeing is more than just an auratic sort of component.

JT It's a base kind of analogy to exposure time, right? I remember, in photography class, that the process of exposure was illustrated with a glass gradually getting filled up with water.

JP Yeah. Those people peeing are the quality of that photograph ... literally, because they've got the light. That's what I was trying to think about, trying to understand: how does the auratic operation work? Where, exactly, does it happen? Is it a space that people need to project on? Is it the space of the absurd? How do you even talk about these sorts of things now?

JT I think it's interesting that something like the auratic only comes into view when it's seemingly disappearing, or somehow threatened. That, effectively, is what it is: it's the quality of something in transition.

JP I was working with Jeremy [Gilbert-Rolfe] at the time, and getting an earful of this whole idea of the presence of absence, all this bullshit about how things can only be read through their absences, and so on.[39] If you stare at blue long enough, it's going to make you think things you don't know how to think, or things you don't know how to talk about thinking about—it's all the same bullshit. At the end of the day, if I can't talk about standing in front of a fucking blue picture, there's something wrong, you know what I mean? It's not any different than saying, you know, the dust in people's hands gives human qualities to chairs, or something like that. It's the same fucking problematic.

39 Jeremy Gilbert-Rolfe was an influential presence at Art Center College of Design from 1986, when he was hired to develop the school's MFA program, until 2015, the year of his retirement. As an artist, he has maintained a lifelong investment in abstract painting. As a teacher and author, he has consistently adhered to a complicated formalist position—working through its early German Romantic roots through to its poststructuralist rethinking in France—in opposition to any issue-driven mode of production. Hence Pardo's mention of "the presence of absence," which, although it is put here in somewhat reductive terms, was a point of fascination for Gilbert-Rolfe.

JT   I'm more inclined to believe the latter, though—that there is something transmissible...

JP   ...I don't believe in either.

JT   But there is something. You can tell the difference between something handmade and a non-handmade thing.

JP   I agree that you can tell the difference; that's not what we're talking about.

JT   It's a kind of warmth I'm talking about.

JP   Warmth? I think the things you make are the things you make. There are just these very straightforward connections to people; you remember them.

JT   Looking at an object, being able to see what kinds of decisions someone made, even if they were bad decisions, sometimes especially if they were bad decisions, there's a certain kind of empathy that's generated there.

JP   Maybe it's more, like, there's a clearer sense of the circuitry, of the economy of desire, when things are made by hand. There's a kind of clarity and a kind of efficiency in the circuitry of desire...

JT   ...It becomes legible, or something.

JP   Not legible, because it's still there. It's all there. These questions of the auratic, they always have a little bit of the snake-oil...

JT   ...I think that they're questions that are designed to make other questions appear. Again, the auratic is this thing that doesn't pre-exist the moment of its disappearance; it only comes into being when something else happens, right? Before mass production, there was no such thing as the auratic, or anything that could go by that name. So it's something that only comes into being then, but it's also something that is made to get you to think past that stage, which then becomes an intermediate stage.

JP Well, then I don't think that's an appropriate use of the word. I think that the auratic always implies that there's something a priori going on. You know, auras are not things that get used provisionally because they don't really work. You can say that auras are something that enter the space of impermanence because they happen when a bunch of other things are brought together, but you don't really need that space. You don't need the auratic, this sense of wonder, all that kind of stuff—you don't need any of it for things to be interesting. It's occlusion, you know what I mean? Things are fucking interesting enough.

JT Sure, but I think the thing that is interesting about the auratic comes into being at such an ambivalent point. Its value is not in nostalgia, for instance; it's not something to be nostalgic about. It's merely a quality that becomes evident when another quality takes over.

JP I understand, I understand ... I understand that a lot of people have put their philosophical chips into eliminating these notions of nostalgia, but then still bringing back the unknowable within a contemporary network of events. That's what Lyotard is on about, and it's fucking unreadable.

JT Basically, I agree. I agree with both of your statements.

JP Ultimately, it's a conservative reading.

JT Well, you know, all of this stuff arcs back to the way in which aesthetic values take over what were formerly religious values.

JP I don't believe that. Like I said at the beginning of our discussion, you can look to the sixties as a model for ways of dealing with these kinds of shifts without a sense of loss. That's the way you do it, because a whole new field comes into play, a whole new set of ...

JT ... It's true, but, again, I think that in order to begin to describe that field, you have to assert some sort of a precedent, which is the auratic to some extent.

JP I think we can all agree that the auratic isn't productive. Not even as a working term, as you're trying to describe it: that it is only present through the absence of this component, or that you don't have the issue of the auratic in objects until machines start to make objects, and people stop.

JT   Maybe it's because the new object, the new technology, can only be talked about, initially, in negative terms. Like, it's never this, this *thing* that is auratic; instead, the auratic is what it no longer is.

JP   I think that the reason people talk about it that way is because they don't know how the new thing works. So, anytime you have new technology, you have a very small group of experts. As that technology opens up, more and more people begin to engage in it, and not just on an elemental level. My nephews, for instance, they're programming stuff; they're not just operating software any longer.

JT   There's people that use it but, at the same time, history, the practice of the historian, is generally devoted to the attempt to come to some sort of understanding of the present state by looking at where it came from, or defining it through what it once was and no longer is. There's value in historical thinking.

JP   There's no value in historical lineage; there's value in historical *thinking*. History is interesting in that it allows us to make comparisons, to compare structural tendencies, to describe in time, through time. But history as an ideological entity is utterly useless.

JT   Well, inasmuch as it's a way to come to grips with what's presently available to us by way of what's no longer available, to describe the difference…

JP   …I think that, on one level, you want to understand why this thing has this particular shape, and so you've got to look at the history of how it was made, how it was projected upon historically. That has nothing to do with saying that history is an anthropomorphization that lives along with us and sits in this chair, you know? That's just a bunch of shit that's written about. There's just as much that's not written about.

JT   The assertion of the auratic is clearly that some part of history is being materialized now, and it's happening at the same time as it is being discarded.

JP   It's all about Presence with a capital P …

JT   … But still a complicated presence.

JP   It's like an index; at the end of the day, it's a database. The great thing about new technology is that everything that was put forward after computers is on a totally different kind of calendar. A totally different sense of time is inscribed in the new information. It makes it clear that even when you plug in the most intimate forms of historical data, this new database will have completely eradicated any possibility of auratic discussion.

JT   I'm doing this class right now called "Allegories of Information," and it's looking from Benjamin to media theorists like Marshall McLuhan and then Friedrich Kittler or Paul Virilio—the poststructuralists. It's basically a historical survey, or an attempt to see how information technology serves history, or not. In this context, it's interesting to bring up someone like Nietzsche, who makes this very sort of partial statement: "Our writing instruments are also working on our thoughts."[40] He means by this that our technology is also writing us, and the "also" is important here because it continues to leave room for some sort of human essence. Then you have someone like Kittler, who is just completely this technological determinist: there is no more human, there is no such thing as consciousness, and so on and so forth—he talks about "so-called humanity." It's all an illusion that's generated by language and it becomes impossible as machines grow increasingly intelligent. So, clearly, in a relatively short period of time, we come to the end of a certain idea about intentionality and consciousness and memory and whatever else might constitute human being. But, at the same time, all of those people are involved in a very intentional sort of periodizing, as if it's absolutely necessary to back up the discussion in order to have anything interesting to say about this new technology at the end of the day. There's always this step back into, at least, the just-past. Because when you're right there, you're simply using, you can't articulate anything …

40   Nietzsche wrote this in a letter to a friend shortly after purchasing his Malling-Hansen Writing Ball typewriter in 1881. The instrument compensated for his failing eyesight, turning him into "the first mechanized philosopher," according to Kittler. See Friedrich A. Kittler, *Gramophone, Film, Typewriter*, trans. Geoffrey Winthrop-Young and Michael Wutz (Stanford, CA: Stanford University Press, 1999), 200.

Fig. 14 *New Work* exhibition, 1990. Installation view, Thomas Solomon's Garage, Los Angeles.

Fig. 15a *Tecoh*, 2006–11, Yucatan, Mexico.

Fig. 15b *Tecoh*, 2006–11, Yucatan, Mexico.

Fig. 15c *Tecoh*, 2006–11, Yucatan, Mexico.

JP You're using but, at the end of the day, how you've been used by the desire to know something is not something that you can factor in. I agree with Nietzsche that our tools of inscription also make up our thoughts but, again, that's not something that we have any sort of calculus for. What's always interested me in Benjamin was never this problem of the auratic; it was this other thing … He was engaged in the problem of writing in the present.

JT But that's just it: using history very consciously for present-day purposes. Seeking out those present-day objects and spaces where history concretely accrues …

JP … Take the *Arcades Project* …

JT … A project that essentially begins with him walking into an abandoned mall, walking into this accretion of the just-past—this "fossil," as he puts it.

JP Within the notes, there's a prognostication that maybe this book is never going to be finished because, ultimately, this lack of finish is going to give it an acuity in regard to history that something complete and reworked could never have. Ultimately, I think that that kind of problematic—the problematic of the unfinished, the problematic of trying to locate where the thing starts and stops—is everything that I'm interested in. To bring it back to the beginning of our discussion: where does the work end?

JT But I think that what we're talking about here is, rather, Where does it begin? I still think that it's salient that, for Benjamin, the whole process starts in this abandoned mall. So he's effectively looking at something …

JP … He's looking at something dead. History.

JT Exactly, but its ruins allow him to look at the present. There is precisely a kind of psychic content, there, in this abandoned architecture that relates to a collective unconscious, if you want. Something like a repressed desire or a wish is working its way through these forms, as he says, "belatedly"—that's his term, I think, or maybe Adorno's.

JP That's a part of Benjamin that I'm not interested in. I think that's where, ultimately, he becomes conservative.

JT I think this step backwards is crucial; it's what gains him any sense of purchase on the present.

JP I don't think so.

JT Because, in the end, he constructs a book that goes way beyond anything the Surrealists had done. It's a database, as you say.

JP It's one of the most progressive forms of fiction in the twentieth century; you can read that book like you read *Ulysses* or something.

JT You're really talking about it in terms of form, of a kind of forwardly moving process, but that doesn't account for his rethinking of archaeology, this notion that there's an archaeology of the present, or even the future.

JP At some point, I think he must have left that idea behind. Archeology doesn't really give you much in your ability to navigate the world. He was looking for a way of talking about what was happening, what was happening in his head at the time. He wasn't doing history.

JT No, but the thing about archaeology is that it literally deals with that part, that concrete part, of history that survives into the present. In that sense, it is very much like thought, which is itself comprised of memories, ruins of experience.

JP I know. I understand that. I understand your point about the ruin, and the origin of the *Arcades Project* in an empty mall, but, like I said, when I think about Benjamin, I don't find those to be the most progressive aspects of his work. And I don't necessarily think that this is something that you have to totalize in any way, particularly in making art. If you're going to use somebody in bits and pieces, then Benjamin is kind of ideal.

JT Yes, and there is a real interest, there, in being useful. A book like that is very interested in its own particular use value. Still, to me, it's a very salient point, this thing about belatedness as a way to imagine the present.

JP   That motion is ultimately what constitutes the postmodern: all these kinds of aggressive moves of redeployment of things that are completely inconsequential in terms of how they relate to the present. I don't think we've left anything behind for the future; I don't think it's useful to think about things that way. Things don't need to get resurrected.

JT   I think that when you look at his philosophy as something that is, on any level, positivistic or providing some notion of what *should* be in the present, I think you run into problems. Of course, with Benjamin, there is more of an interest in describing a kind of negativity, literally a negative image.

JP   I think that most people who use Benjamin use him because he is very efficient in that way of projecting the world. Benjamin is used as a Marxist, not necessarily as a lunatic. In actuality, though, he's much closer to Nietzsche than he is to Marx.

JT   Actually, he spent most of his time waffling between ideologies, and I'm interested in how that kind of waffling is very productive in his own work. On the one hand, there's the model of Surrealism, which suggests one way of navigating the city and the unconscious, and then, of course, there's "vulgar" Marxism. On one side, then, he retreats with Freud and [André] Breton into the space of the private and the intimate, whereas, on the other, he has to imagine the world stage and the historical stage as the space of action or something. You know, these two very different dimensions of thought are emerging simultaneously at a certain point ...

JP   ... They depend on one another. With Nietzsche, you have the need for the master narrative; with Freud, you have the master narrative that's plugged into the intimate; and with Marx, it's plugged into the public, and you also have this little machine going, "It's good to be poor," or else, "It's not good." How good is good, historically? You know, look at what's happening: it's like, "We have to think about ourselves, because if we don't, we're not going to pay people enough money." You need psychoanalysis so that you're not sadistic, right? You know, psychoanalysis is this total attack on sadism, and if you don't get rid of sadism, then there's no Marxism—in Marx, there's just no room for it. Then you have Nietzsche, the great Dionysian ... and that's nothing if not sadism.

JT Right: the imposition of the will—a blind will.

JP How much more sadistic can you be than that?

JT You could look at Marxism as this massive sublimation, right? Yeah, all that's very interesting in relation to sadism. I'm really eager to talk this over some more.

JP Then we'll do a TV show!

JT Sounds great ...

11

SITE-SPECIFICITY
PORTRAITURE
CLIENT RELATIONS

Los Angeles
October 24, 2012

Almost a decade had elapsed between conversations. In the course of working on the *Tecoh* project, Jorge had basically moved his studio operation to Mexico. Once this work was completed, however, he came back to town for a time, setting up shop in a former post office in the El Sereno neighborhood of East L.A., where he also lived, having vacated 4166 Sea View Lane following his divorce. As mentioned in the introduction to this book, I was then working on an essay about *Tecoh*, and I wanted to ask him how this work might be situated in relation to the legacies of land art and earthworks, as well as the more general idea of art as a destination. This conversation mainly circles around problems of siting; Jorge remains notably sanguine throughout it. "Generally, I'm much more interested in things that one leaves behind," he states at one point, which suggests to me that these things become interesting when they are left in a particular place, and remain there, but also when he himself has left this place and these things.

JT Writing about you in the introduction to his new book [*The Trans-Disciplinary Studio*], Alex Coles mentions the Daniel Buren essay, "The Function of the Studio," and what Buren describes as "the unspeakable compromise of the portable work of art."[41] That, of course, is a tract pushing a neo-avant-garde, post–Conceptual, institutional critique position. But it's also a fairly old fashioned idea: that works of art should exist in and for specific places. I came

41 Daniel Buren, "The Function of the Studio," *October* 10 (Autumn 1979): 54. In this essay, which Buren wrote in 1971, he recounts his early experience of elation while visiting a series of painter's studios throughout southeastern France, and then his corresponding disappointment upon seeing their works installed in galleries and museums. "This sense that the main point of the work is lost somewhere between its place of production and place of consumption forced me to consider the problem and the significance of the work's place." Buren, 56. "The Function of the Studio" can be read as an origin story for Buren's own practice, his ongoing attempt to circumvent the compromised role of the discrete artwork by instead working *in situ*.

across this point recently in Goethe's writing, where he argues that, in the past, artworks have always been rooted to a specific locality.[42] This is obvious in the case of civic sculpture, as well as religious art, which is made for churches, and often made inside those churches, and if you want to see it, you have to go to those churches, to make a pilgrimage. Anyway, Alex refutes the Buren post–studio argument and tries to propose a new model of what the studio is, or could be. In your case, he discusses the notion of the transplanted, satellite studio, or a studio that can actually operate on-site, taking advantage of the local materials, workmanship, and aesthetic sensibilities.[43] The mobility of the studio maybe allows the work to participate more closely in the culture of the place it will eventually wind up in.

JP Well, that's an old notion, isn't it? It starts to change a bit with the Grand Tour and all that. Stuff starts to get moved around and decontextualized. Then it becomes an object that has a whole different set of rules in terms of how you project its history, and how you project its history in relationship to some impropriety as a result of displacing it (*laughs*). Generally, I'm much more interested in things that one leaves behind. There's the things that you make in the studio, there's the things that you sell, but at the end of the day the things that are the most engaging are present in a particular place to which I have to respond for an extended period of time.

JT The extended period of time is key, right? Because we've already had the opening up of the space of production to the art fairs and the biennials and to projects made on those sites. But typically these involve a more superficial attempt to generate a concept about the place that you're in, because you're there for just a short stay. All of that stuff *really* does get left behind.

42 "The location of works of art has always been of the greatest importance to the cultivation of artists, as well as the enjoyment of amateurs. There was a time when, with few exceptions, they usually remained in their proper place and setting. Now a great change has taken place which cannot fail to have important consequences for art in general and in particular." J. W. von Goethe, "Introduction to Propyläen" (1798), *Goethe on Art*, ed. John Gage (London: Scolar Press, 1980), 15.

43 Around 2006, Pardo recreated a substantial part of his Los Angeles studio in Mérida, Mexico, to work on his project *Tecoh*. Since 2012, he has made Mexico his operational base, closing up shop on the West Coast.

JP Well, the other concept that exists in those venues is the point of purchase concept, and that's really what overrides everything else in the art fair: it's for sale first and it's for sale last.

JT I'm thinking of those projects where you have what's been termed "visiting artists" attempting to be site-specific, but they're on a tight schedule, and really only cobbling something together.

JP There's always all kinds of problems with these shows in the sense that there's an underlying narrative that nobody really gets at: a big part of these pieces is how they are going to transport themselves into an economic liability. In other words, these things are provisional, but their aspiration is to be collected. So, in the end, they are different, but not so different.

JT They get uprooted...

JP ...They get uprooted for reasons that are actually quite interesting, but at the end of the day, I don't think that that circumstance of the work has any kind of critical traction. The issue is how do you sell something like that to a collector, and what's the collector's notion of it being reappropriated into domesticity or some sort of a private scenario? And that kind of operation is mired with all sorts of fucked up problems, because if you want to talk about site and you don't talk about its motion, and how it's driven by a very significant value-added function, then you're really not talking about the work.

JT Your Yucatán project, *Tecoh* (fig. 15a, b, c), is maybe the most public project you've done?

JP I think the Münster pier (fig. 6) is extremely public. It was going to be temporary, but it stayed; it's been there for fifteen years. I've never made a pier for anyone else; it has never been installed anywhere else.

JT That was all about a juxtaposition of these building materials associated with mid-century California with a German landscape...

JP ...Or just associated with California. It's not really a mid-century structure; it's a little more awkward than that. But anyway it's different now: it's made of German oak. The California redwood, it rotted *(laughs)*, and the city decided that they liked the pier to some degree, and they wanted to keep it, so they used a harder wood.

JT   So that's your first really public piece?

JP   Probably. But when I talk about works that propose a very rigorous relation to a charged site, it's often about how, because they were there, they become much more valuable, and then their final destination is elsewhere. These shows are basically 3D PR. Everybody pretends to talk about this work as if it were in a neutral condition, but it isn't; it's just as commercial as anything else. I'd say it's even more commercial because the condition of their being there is all about adding value to the work. When it finally does arrive at its destination, it's usually private.

JT   Adding value to the work, but sometimes to the site as well, when it becomes a destination.

JP   If it stays…

JT   But that is also the function of the biennial, where the work doesn't stay.

JP   Yes, the work has a national presence. These really are venues that model a certain kind of nationalistic *goodness* *(laughs)*, and they are a measure of how a nation values its culture.

JT   Yes, and for certain perhaps less developed nations and cities, the biennial becomes a gateway to a larger marketplace. You attract tourists, certainly an upper echelon of tourists.

JP   And you develop a collector class that's local. A James Turrell, or something like that, operates very differently in its relation to the site. The money goes to one place; it works to intensify that place.

JT   Such works were often placed in sites that are remote—I'm thinking here of Michael Heizer's *Double Negative*, or Smithson's *Spiral Jetty*. There's no significant revenue that can be generated from earthworks, at least not touristically.

JP They're in the middle of nowhere. You almost don't see them; that's the reality of these works. I don't necessarily think it's more real or anything like that. But when something is placed in a pavilion in Venice, let's say, it tends to be very instructional in developing some notion of site-specificity. It's just assumed that the destination of the work is there, when really it isn't. The site is just an extension of the marketplace.

JT **What were you thinking by siting a California aesthetic in Münster with your pier project?**

JP Oh, I was interested in this notion of representing everything around me. I was trying to understand the representational limits of an aspiration like that—like, what *wouldn't* come across? When you do that in a place like Münster, you propose a whole set of problems that are in this awkward state of suspension. How do you take one place and put it into another? Can you use the distance between one place and another to talk about how difficult it is to ground the work in the local? Is site-specificity conducive to representation? In the tradition of that sort of work, is it like a pipe dream to think that it can speak representationally like a painting does, or like a figurative sculpture?

JT **On the subject of pipe dreams, you included a cigarette dispenser at the end of your pier.**

JP Well, a pier is always a place of commerce, sometimes more crudely than others. Traditionally, it's a place where materials come and go, but when it's in a bucolic setting like this one, it's basically a place of pleasure.

JT **And here the pleasure has to do with taking in the site. In that sense, the pier is a kind of optical device.**

JP Yeah, and I thought it would be interesting to put a kind of non sequitur into that because cigarettes make smoke, they make atmosphere, so it was a very rude way of referencing the bucolic. I remember that Michael Asher was walking around before the show opened, and I happened to be on the pier, and he was on the pier, and he looked at me kind of funny and said, "Why did you do this? Why did you make a pier? Why did you put a cigarette machine in it?" And I was thinking that this guy is really a piece of work. I said, "Michael, you've always got to keep the bucolic at arm's length."

JT   And you're a smoker, so this idea of representing everything around you is also in a way to represent yourself.

JP   But what I was interested in is at what point does this notion of representing the artist fall apart? Can there be a material representation of that falling apart? It begins as an eccentric form of portraiture: it's this portraiture where you can't tell what you're seeing, who you are, what you're making and where it's going to go...

JT   Alex [Coles] pointed out the reproduction of *Las Meniñas* that you have in your house in Mérida, perhaps to suggest the centrality of portraiture as a genre in your work, regardless of what sorts of objects you actually wind up producing.[44] That painting in particular foregrounds the person of the artist and the mediation he undertakes with his patron or client.

JP   It's sloppy; it's interesting. It is the first image that, in a modern sense, has some real critical traction. Who is this painting for? It's a question that transports itself into documentary filmmaking, or any kind of intersubjective enterprise where you have to work *with* somebody and not just for somebody or for yourself. And then how much of yourself gets traced in it, and, as a producer, how do you measure that? Can it be embedded into an object, a material, a place?

44 "An eight-hundred-dollar copy of Diego Velázquez's *Las Meniñas* (1656), executed by local artisan Jesus Chucho, hangs in the reception room-cum-micro-studio of Jorge Pardo's private house in Mérida, the Yucatán. The painting is the very image of self-reflexivity—nothing less than a representation of the classical form of representation itself ... The dynamic established here between the image of the painter working in his makeshift studio, his subject, and the viewer, is then telescoped through the mirror at the back of the room in which the scene takes place. The reflection of the mirror produces what Foucault refers to as 'a metathesis of visibility.' And it's surely the painting's capacity to produce this metathesis—an additional commentary on the mechanics of representation—that has caused Pardo to commission the copy and hang it in such a prominent position in the first place." Alex Coles, *The Transdisciplinary Studio* (Berlin: Sternberg Press, 2012), 25.

JT Not having seen the *Tecoh* project, but having read about it and heard you talk about it, it sounds a little different to the pier in that you're dealing so closely with local craftspeople and local materials. And then the whole project, to some extent, is an attempt to preserve some of the local culture and history ...

JP ... Preserve, but also represent some of the problems of preserving, because I don't think we were at all interested in any sort of historical fidelity.

JT OK, but the project begins with the site, which has a certain amount of historical information already in it, and which you didn't raze. You have these ruins of a former industry that you left in place, and then worked around. In that sense, the work functions almost like a casing, or vitrine.

JP We didn't work around them, really; it's more like sticking something on them. And it's not really about framing the problems that might result from any perceived abuse of their history either, but trying to use the more aesthetic aspects of that history. This could be anything from the particular stylistic tendencies a hacienda originated with, like the shape of the arches—are they designed in relation to organic forms, or something else?—or it could have to do with a redeployment of traditional methods of building that make a place really comfortable to be in. I was interested in the opulence of the things that are from there more than anything else. How do you direct that into a palette of some sort? That region is so charged historically that it's almost tragic to propose a reframing of it.

JT So the aesthetic aspects of that history are mobilized, but to what end?

JP *Tecoh* is really more about a relationship that occurred between myself and my patrons, Roberto Hernandez and Claudia Madrazo. If you want to understand why it is the way it is, you would probably have to start there. It's impossible for one to have an indifferent relationship with what's going on—socially, economically, politically—in the Yucatán, but I didn't want this to determine the entire physiognomy of the work. This is a very strange project that couldn't have been conceived programmatically. It doesn't really know what it wants to be.

JT Right, but didn't it initially have some sort of civic mandate? To attract people from elsewhere to the region, and to somehow acquaint them with the local culture and history? Wasn't there talk, early on, of an instructional garden display, for instance, with each indigenous plant named and described?

JP We avoided all that.

JT Because it's sentimental?

JP Because it's sentimental, but also because it totalizes a program that is no program (*laughs*). We're not really sure what it's for, and that is not something that I'm really interested in prescribing.

JT So you started with one plan and then moved on to another. You started building and then changed course, all the while discussing what the building is for…

JP …The question is, how does a building become discursive.

JT And here we're talking about the process of building as integral to that discursive function. It is not only a matter of design in the predetermined sense, where this function would be conceived here and then executed there, say, in one fell swoop. In *Tecoh*, you are thinking through the hands-on process of making.

JP It's processional, and not obsessed with totality.

JT So you could change your mind at any point, and tear some part of it down and start over?

JP We tore lots of things down; we rebuilt them; we changed things as we could, but all within reason.

JT On the more unreasonable side, I think of an analogy to the Winchester Mystery House, for instance.[45] Having a generous budget certainly helps, because this isn't the most efficient way to work, right?

JP That's part of what makes those conditions possible, but more importantly than that, it has to do with the comfort level of the patron to see this process as productive. There are all kinds of architectural projects that have a similar methodology, but they are mostly follies. If you look at how *Tecoh* is structured, the buildings always bear a relation to one another, while not necessarily marshaling toward a final programmatic end. The most interesting thing about it is that it never had a program, because places like this, are generally built around a program.

JT   You're terming the project "processional" because it foregrounds the process of its making, but also because there is a procession involved of one thing, one building, after another...

JP   ...And also because we were simply trying to understand how to build in the Yucatán. There were all these limitations, and the longer we worked on the project, the more we started to infuse our studio practices and building methodologies into these. So there was a folding of the studio into the site that was real because it produced a second order of complications that had to be negotiated. Something as simple as a floor panel or three-dimensional tile we'd prototype ourselves and then have it manufactured locally. And you could see these things were different, but that the one could still be threaded through the other, through that kind of localized, indigenous craft.

JT   This interaction seems also partly to play into the original plan for *Tecoh*, that it serves to somehow revitalize the local economy?

JP   The relation of the Hernandez's to the Yucatán has always been philanthropic—philanthropic with an educational thrust, and with a sober relationship to economic sustainability. They went down there because they fell in love with the region and then they started to buy up all these haciendas, and they were trying to figure out a way to preserve them. And one way you do that is turn the hacienda into a hotel, and they found that, in a town of

45 The so-called Winchester Mystery House is a sprawling mansion in San Jose, California, that was the residence of Sarah Lockwood Pardee Winchester, heiress to the fortune of the famous arms manufacturer. Starting out as an eight-room farmhouse, it underwent almost continuous construction, between 1886 and 1922, ultimately expanding to 160 rooms. This architectural oddity survives mainly as a tourist destination. I cite it as a popular and highly eccentric instance of what Pardo terms a "processional" relation to building—that is, building without a plan.

200 people, or something like that, it completely transforms the economy.

JT **Right, but in a particular way.**

JP In a very particular way: into a service economy. They had used that model several times before, but when they got to me, I said I'm not so interested in that model. I don't have a problem with it; I think it's a very rational model, but I want to work with their program a little more eccentrically. I think that ultimately the sustainability of *Tecoh* will have to do with what it can produce discursively. And, by the way, there's forty or fifty people that work in this place, and those people have jobs now with the sort of regularity that didn't exist before. It's become a place for symposia mostly. I'll spend a week there with my students from Princeton; LACMA did a retreat for their curators there; the Hernandez's will gather their friends from the banking or historic preservation worlds there. It's a place where you go with a particular topic, and then you disperse that topic within the place, which always returns you to the question of why is this place here?

12

FRAGILITY
ART CRITICISM
POLITICAL ART
POST-IDEALISM
BEAUTY

Los Angeles
November 2, 2012

It was Jorge who proposed art criticism as the subject of this conversation. Right after the conclusion of the last one, he suggested that we turn our attention to the writings of Benjamin H. D. Buchloh and Dave Hickey, sending me off with some reading homework. Reconsidering this proposal now, I cannot help but think that it was another one of those events that he regularly sets up to get the most out of his friends, while also "responding to the conditions of the day we are speaking," as he puts it near the end of this book. It was a solid plan: to consider the polarized relation of these two critics could offer a shorthand summation of the problems that we had been confronting over the years, problems always circling in one way or another around the place of aesthetics in politics, and vice versa. Also, possibly, such a comparative study might open a way out of the condition of ideological gridlock that we both experienced while in school, and that still showed no sign of subsiding. As a background note, both of us attended art school at the end of the eighties, CalArts in my case and Art Center College of Design in his. At CalArts in those years, Buchloh was unavoidable, cropping up in one syllabus after another, whereas Art Center would probably have been more favorably inclined toward Hickey. We are digging up some ancient history here.

JT   Reading over Alex Cole's recent interviews with you, I was struck by the consistency of your thoughts. Your ideas haven't really changed that much since we began our conversation, but the way you articulate them has. There are certain words that you now privilege, such as "fragility," which is related to "contingency" or "the poetic," perhaps, but then also is different.[46] I'm curious about how you settle

46 See Alex Coles and Jorge Pardo, "Dialogue, Part 1: Fragility," *Jorge Pardo: Tecoh* (Berlin: Sternberg Press, 2012), 84–102.

on these particular words, and what purpose they serve in relation to your practice. These words are part of a discourse, they describe what you make, but they can also influence what you make.

JP Right, and they do. There are not a lot of texts written about my work, but there are a fair number of interviews, and, most of the time, when somebody sets out to write about my work, they use these interviews. The word "fragility" came out of an insistence on Alex's part that the artist have a discourse component in their practice.[47] For most of the artists of my generation, at least those who are around at present, the theory almost functions as an index to extract, to produce, to collate and congeal the work. Alex was always frustrated that I don't really take charge of something like that, and that's where it started. Because I'm interested instead in things that are much more *fragile*, this idea that the viewing, the reception and the presence are what constitutes the work.

JT This could feed into your suggestion that we talk a little bit about art criticism today, starting with the writings of Benjamin Buchloh. He obviously descends from a line of critics that chart a historical arc in the evolution of modern art to the present. This arc is to some extent modeled on avant-garde precedents that can be traced back to the Russian Constructivists, for instance, and to their insistence on a certain kind of straightforwardness in the production of works, and also to their insistence on the anaesthetic, or a type of aesthetic that does not have a mythical component, the Romantic "genius" component. Instead it's about an ideal of transparency, so that people understand exactly how a work is made, and can then make it themselves if they want to, or derive a method of making from it. Buchloh subscribes to that model on the one hand, but he also subscribes to the Duchampian model, a very different model of the anaesthetic that has more to do with a denial of taste and the alienation effects that result. Moreover, Duchamp considered viewership an individual act, or at least a less collective one. At any rate, Buchloh proceeds from Constructivism and Duchamp to an

47 "I want to begin these dialogues with an issue that has bugged me for some time. There's a conceptual density to the way you conceive of your work … And yet the visually playful language you have developed to deal with these conceptual issues belies this density—which many viewers can't get past. Have you ever considered choreographing the viewer toward the issues you are concerned with in a more deliberate way?" Coles and Pardo, 84.

artist like Michael Asher, and there you have this arc of a critical art that winds up looking a certain way. Basically, it has to pare away all those components that you embrace in your work—components that are not just "fragile," you could call them frivolous too. Maybe that's what Alex was also responding to: your insistence on a *particular* aesthetic. It has a relation to the beautiful, whether it really is beautiful or not, and it is added on to the things you make, perhaps obscuring, or complicating, what you have termed their "critical traction."

JP What I always found problematic with the efficiencies of an argument like Buchloh's is that it has to disregard a lot of things; it has to stay on track. First of all, to even attempt that kind of linearity is already problematic. Obviously, he's using a communist model to argue for an art that is specific and clear about its material use, and so, unless you extract the more complicated and less clear kinds of motions—let's say the decorative, or the flourish—the work goes astray. It stops being scientific; it can't be used politically. A simple way to read Buchloh is to say that the works he champions are works that, in their production, model a mechanism that one can use to look at other things in one's life, and apply. In the process, one gains an awareness, a kind of emancipatory condition that comes from looking at things one is not normally supposed to see.

JT Right, and, as you've mentioned, that relates to a communist model, because the event of emancipation can, in this case, only be imagined in a collective–normative sense ...

JP It's always a matter of extracting the general from the specific, and that doesn't seem to always work. There are so many forces in the work's riveting structure that are, to some degree, indifferent to that—for instance, the way that photography operates in a project like Asher's. Photography is never talked about that much; it is never really tethered to the work. You never discuss aesthetic concerns in regard to how a Michael Asher is actually reproduced, and yet the primary consumption of his works is through their reproduction. And there's a lot of drama in that. There's a kind of Romantic urgency that the images and texts need to have, and there's a kind of determinism in their need to champion this over that. It is still very much rooted in the problem of taste and value.

The title of Buchloh's essay on Asher, "The Conclusion of Modernist Sculpture," is highly romantic, and it points to a very specific selection process by somebody who is discerning.

JT   It's a complicated argument. It begins with the example of Constructivism, which is where sculpture becomes detached from the tradition of carving and modeling, and starts to use standardized, mass-produced materials. It starts to participate in the industrial collectivization of labor ...

JP   ... There is the imposition of a neutrality on these materials because they are culturally available to do other things with, but people have always been using stone for other things, and steel for other things. So, this is just about attributing a condition of modernist enthusiasm to these materials.

JT   And that condition existed at one time.

JP   It did, and it was mostly manifest in architecture, in construction. But if you're going to base your argument on a very handicapped notion of how to read these materials, those readings will only be culturally valuable for a short period of time. Nobody thinks of steel that way anymore, or Plexiglas.

JT   True, but there is, in the writing, an understanding of the naivety of that early enthusiasm for the material, and also an appreciation for the utopian thrust of the sculptor who works with it. Buchloh's argument then turns to the postwar appropriation of Constructivist modes of fabrication by Minimalism, but now outside any sort of utopian framework—a representative instance might be Dan Flavin's *Monument to Tatlin*. At that point, the materials, even though store-bought and generic, start to get aestheticized, and they start to take on the sorts of flourishes you mentioned—the visible signs of a particular sensibility.

JP   The particularity of one's appropriation of those materials, which again brings up the relation of the specific and the poetic in the configuration of the work.

JT   So, Buchloh begins with Constructivism and then moves on to its corrupt return—the corrupt, postwar, American appropriation of materials and methodologies once charged with utopian ideals. This bleak historical account, which constitutes the bulk of his essay, finally turns to Asher, who ostensibly affects its redemption, but he can only do so to an extent, because he is now operating within a corrupted context. So, these types of gestures we're talking about, although they have been deaestheticized, or somewhat anaestheticized, are now answering to the very particular context of the museum, and to its very limited audience.

JP   And also there is a myth that runs through that account, and this is the myth of economic neutrality. These artists not only delimit a field of operation, but limit the work's relationship to consumption through what they choose to do and how they choose to do it. It's very hard to own a Daniel Buren, and it's almost impossible to own a Michael Asher, and that condition lends itself to a neutral reading, which I don't think is adequate to what really happens. Those contingencies that these artists exploit to limit the reception of their works, they become just as subjective as anything else. But even if one tries to argue that these artists deploy very eccentric methods of denial and restriction to precisely determine just how a work is to be constituted every time it's shown, or not shown, they are so tethered to temporal issues that they really don't exist outside their duration. And somehow that aspect of it gets threaded back into some sense of neutrality. A person like me doesn't read things that way, because I'm obsessed with the problematic details. I'm obsessed with what one actually does to get to that place. In the end, Buchloh's argument is not really that different from Greenberg's: it is there to lend a substantive historical thrust to choices made for very personal reasons.

JT   In the introduction to his collection of writings on the neo-avant-garde, Buchloh basically admits to it—that is, to what extent his critical sensibility was shaped by the historical context of growing up in postwar Germany and being schooled in a very limited, and highly politicized, range of ideas on art.[48] At the time, it was all about the artist as a "cultural worker," someone always on the side of the collective. The artist is the producer of a surplus value that is emancipatory, but you're saying that it actually benefits more the one percent who can afford their work.

48 See Benjamin H. D. Buchloh, "Introduction," *Neo-Avantgarde and Culture Industry: Essays on European and American Art from 1955 to 1975* (Cambridge, MA: MIT Press, 2000), xvii–xxxiii.

JP   Well, the more that work is somehow *naughty* to that one percent—because it can't really be rude, or aggressive, or disconnected—the more convincing it is to someone like him. But, at the end of the day, these are just ensembles of resistance, and I use the word "ensembles" because it's a *play* (*laughs*). It's not changing anything; if anything, it's fueling the conditions it wants to oppose. Works become more expensive, not less, and fewer people actually get to own them, not more. These applied art moves become increasingly distanced from the emancipatory conditions they originally hoped to fulfill. You get images of this now, and you get them framed; it's the job of the critic, the curator, the dealer, or the collector to reconstitute this stuff so that it can then be sustained historically within the institution.

JT   Buchloh would argue that what Asher produces is a form of counter-spectacle, and that this is directed against an institution that is now largely beholden to the so-called culture industry.

JP   As an art student, I thought the opposite happens: Asher's work becomes the polemic of the most spectacular. If you were in school in the eighties, for instance, there was Julian Schnabel and all these painters making a lot of money, and then there was Michael Asher, and the fact that his work sets itself up in a sort of parallax is not because it's a counter-spectacle, but because it's a different type of spectacle. It's the spectacle of the real, the earnest, the good.

JT   In fact, the condition of spectacle as it exists now is much closer to Michael Asher than someone like Richard Serra, whose art Buchloh cites as openly spectacular.

JP   Asher is the person with the largest career who never had a career.

JT   Rereading some of our early conversations, I came across your frequent use of the term "post–idealism." "We live in a post–idealistic age," you say—and I then began to think about what sorts of implications that might have for criticism. Buchloh is certainly an idealistic critic, an ideologue; as mentioned, he comes from the Left, he upholds that notion of a political economy, and he orients his work around those ideals. The artist, in his estimation, has a role to play in the production of a non-alienated collective. On the other hand, we can look at a critic like Dave Hickey, who embodies a whole other political economy with much the same sort of enthusiasm. He has a certain faith in the notion that capitalism is not unfree, that it keeps changing, adapting to new demands, etc., and so, doesn't really pose the threat to art that Buchloh keeps warning against. At any rate, these two critics embody a postwar, or Cold War, opposition, and they are most reductive in their thinking when they are most polemically on point, or when they are at their most idealistic. But, to some extent, that reductive view is necessary to form criteria, and to make judgments of quality that are general, not specific.

JP   But you don't have to reduce in order to see things. It just gets more difficult because you have to parse things out, and you end up with more slices of things to look at in the metric of this other scenario that is more expansive. That is one of the things I'm interested in: how do you make works that are not based on the reductive, on getting rid of the remainder? How do you make works that are full of problems that one is not concerned with managing? This is important because art-making is above all a speculative process. I want to make works not in relation to a general, quantifiable sense of what the public is; I want to make something specific.

JT   The specific is something that changes all the time; it is not beholden to general criteria.

JP   The specific is really about how do you want to slice this thing up? How many parts can this thing have? Buchloh wants to control that operation; he's obsessive-compulsive. And Hickey actually believes that works of art are more real when they swim in the populist stream. I don't necessarily agree with any of that.

JT   But Hickey does propose a somewhat complex argument in regard to what populism is ...

JP   ... Yeah, it's much more complex than Buchloh's. Buchloh basically lives in a cell, and once you are outside of that, his questions become irrelevant. Whereas Hickey maybe takes too much into account.

JT Well, he sees the realm of popular culture—or "the culture industry," in Buchloh's Frankfurt School terms—as one that is not monolithic, but divided into "constituencies of taste," as he puts it. And art, effective art, can function not to cement the connections between people, but to drive them further apart, to actually incite oppositions between them that may in time be worked out. But what's important is that these oppositions become real social events. That is his argument against the institution of art, where every outcome is predetermined, to an extent.

JP You can't have that happening within the institution, but once you lose the institutional frame, nothing happens. I don't think he's way off base; I just have a problem with the works he supports.

JT In his book *The Invisible Dragon*, he sets up an analogy between the work of Caravaggio and Robert Mapplethorpe, whose practice he sees as exemplary. So, on the one hand, this work exists within the institution, but it creates a big problem for the institution as well as the public.

JP I really don't think that it does...

JT ... Well, at one point, Mapplethorpe was at the flashpoint of a political debate, which led to the gutting of the NEA. This is a debate that was not cordoned off from the public.[49]

49 The Corcoran Gallery in Washington, D.C. was scheduled to mount a retrospective exhibition of Robert Mapplethorpe's work in the summer of 1989, just months after the artist's death from AIDS. Unfortunately titled *The Perfect Moment*, the show was canceled due to an outcry from that came mainly from the religious right, who agitated not only against the perceived "obscenity" of Mapplethorpe's frank depictions of gay sexuality, but against the funding of their display by taxpayer dollars. Since the gallery had received a grant from the National Endowment for the Arts, the controversy surrounding the proposed retrospective would in turn lead to a very substantial defunding of that organization, which persists into the present day. Hickey approaches this dismal episode with a measure of optimism—"It was a fine moment," he writes—for in it he observes a real demonstration of art's political efficacy. Hickey mentions the Senator Jesse Helms, who led the charge against Mapplethorpe, as one who at least "understood what Robert was proposing, and took it, correctly, as a direct challenge to everything he believed in." Dave Hickey, *The Invisible Dragon: Four Essays on Beauty* (Los Angeles: Art Issues Press, 1993), 21–22.

JP But the problem is that the debate can never carry the weight, or the density, of the issue. When it enters the public, it just gets reduced. It's basically a Buchloh–like argument that the public performs, and the work becomes instrumental again.

JT But these are two different ideas as to what's monolithic. For Buchloh, it's "the culture industry" that's monolithic because it has been subsumed to an American model, to a corporate model, whereas the institution of art is something that is, for him, still salvageable. It's still part of the public sphere, even if it's not functioning right now.

JP Even though it's never been part of the public sphere ...

JT ... Yeah, it's holding a place.

JP Like a placemat or something ...

JT ... But, for Hickey, it's rather the institution of art that is monolithic and problematic, and this is not because it has been overtaken by the forces of capital, but because it operates on a Socialist model as a kind of top-down legislator of what is good for you.

JP Yeah, the problem is that, in order to make that argument, he has to start pouring his shit in (*laughs*). And then he has to set up criteria which are, in some ways, much more far-fetched than Buchloh's.

JT So, Hickey winds up supporting works that may well be trivial, whereas in the case of Buchloh, it's only works that are self-important. But I am interested in the clarity of these two critical positions, and in the absolute grounding of their criteria. Such grounding becomes impossible, I think, in a post–idealistic age. How does one avoid arbitrary judgments under post–idealistic conditions?

JP I think that the arbitrary has been demonized, when it's just one of the contingencies. The arbitrary becomes the fulcrum on which the work is actually present or not, real or not, successful or not, and that is seen as problematic. But I don't think it's really that detrimental, because everything in the world has these arbitrary components. In other words, I don't think that there is any cultural sphere that can act as a glue to manage that problem. If you want to really look at the problems these critics are posing you have to look at *what* becomes arbitrary in works.

JT   So, an insistence on arbitrariness, on the idea of the arbitrary as well as its working through in a practical sense, could become non-arbitrary over time. It's perhaps what gets carried over and refined from one work to the next.

JP   Yeah, the work always has these remainders within it, and these remainders can attach themselves to different discourses, but I'm interested in a condition where the inception of the work is not driven by any kind of endgame within this polemic. I want something else, something that resists instrumentalizing. If you realize that there is this cultural sphere that the work is part of, and that produces the work to some degree, then let's make some problems for that, so that what gets spat out in the end is closer to questions than answers.

JT   One last point I want to mention about the critical dichotomy we've been sketching out, and about Buchloh's defense of Asher, is that he sees him operating in the realm of "situational aesthetics"—it's a term that comes from Victor Burgin, and it predates Bourriaud's "relational aesthetics"—where the artist adapts their practice to the given conditions of the space, the time, etc., of the exhibition, and takes himself out of this equation as an aesthetic force.[50] So, that, maybe, is the non-arbitrary component within works that are entirely contingent. Now, you've implied that there is, in your own work, a lot of fallout and carry over from one project to the next, and that there's a certain sort of personality that comes into focus over time. Here, then, the artist is someone who makes manifest their particular aesthetic, their taste, or their problem with taste, and that endows this operation with some sort of critical thrust, which maybe comes closer to the Hickey argument.

50   Victor Burgin coined the term "situational aesthetics" in an influential essay from 1969 that bears this title. The term "relational aesthetics" was first proposed by Nicolas Bourriaud in 1996 as a way to link the various artists that he had curated into his exhibition *Traffic* at the CAPC Museum of Contemporary Art in Bordeaux, France. Pardo was included on the roster, alongside Rirkrit Tiravanija, Liam Gillick, and others, all of whom became quickly associated with Bourriaud's term.

JP Buchloh is old school, he's Europe, whereas Hickey is American. Hickey wants art to participate in society, but can only imagine it happening by way of transgression. I think that nothing transgressive is interesting; first of all, because we're not in a place where transgression has any grit in it. We're not ISIS, you know, or any of those cultures that blow themselves up (*laughs*). You can't have transgression within a context where the first priority is to be seen, read, and then to evaluated as positive, great, and bought. Transgression is only possible when you're talking to God, or something like that, because then it becomes totally fucking unmanageable (*laughs*). There's no way you can reorganize it so that it is productive.

JT OK, but you're also interested in the unmanageable. And then, on the other side of the portraiture argument, you've also talked about taking yourself out of the picture, at least in part, and attending more to the contingencies of the patron, the site, the historical moment, and so on. Which then starts to incline toward the situational aesthetics of Burgin and Buchloh.

JP I always make everything I do very explicit; the problem is that I make the *wrong* things explicit—at least, from the Buchloh perspective. I tend to stress an intensity of observation.

JT Right, so your insistence on such things as color and ornament, pattern and decoration—things that touch on the beautiful, at best, and at worst, on the tasteful—complicates the reading of works, perhaps intentionally. To some extent you follow the Buchloh-Asher line by explicitly manifesting all the relations that make the work possible and all the contingencies encountered along the way of its making, but you do it in a way that is not only nonreductive, but openly excessive.

JP There is always an excess. The thing I want to make clear in my work is that you can still perform all those operations, but there is always going to be something left over, something that doesn't gel. And it's not necessarily about beauty as a transgressive category, but more about the frivolous.

JT For Jeremy Gilbert-Rolfe, for instance, the frivolous is antipuritanical. It subverts the value system this culture is founded on; it's powerful in that sense.

JP And, to be honest, it is for me too, although I don't necessarily think it's so powerful as a polemic tool, or in terms of what it's trying to replace its opposite with. What I'm trying to think about is an *extensive* deployment of aesthetic discourse. So, what do you work with? You work with places, with people, with things; you work with painting and sculpture, with landscape and por-traiture; you work with issues of site and representation. It's not about fighting against a reductive modernist–idealist position with excess; I just happen to think that those things are really useful because they are just there. They make themselves present with-out a lot of energy; they are efficient.

13

ART WORLD POLEMICS (CONTINUED)

Los Angeles
November 25, 2012

We return to the subject of aesthetics versus politics; this basically wraps up our last conversation. Jorge aligns himself more with Hickey's position than Buchloh's for reasons that by now are probably obvious, but also because, as he puts it, Hickey is "a little bit crazy." What might become clearer for the reader at this juncture is something that often does not translate between spoken and written words: the egalitarian tone that mitigates even his most pejorative assessments. Everyone in Jorge's world is deemed neurotic in one way or another, but this is not just a way for him to assert his own greater lucidity. In fact, the artists that tend to receive the roundest condemnation—Michael Asher, for one—are actually figures he cares about deeply. As opposed to our previous conversations, which were often held in restaurants while eating, these last three took place in the morning over coffee. After we were done talking, we would join Jorge's production crew at a big table in the studio for a lavish communal meal, prepared by an on-staff cook. I recall feeling some animosity from the artist's chief assistant and fabricator, James Randall, at these gatherings, and later learned that he was still upset by a piece I had written many years earlier in which I characterized Jorge's work as shoddily made. This was not meant as an insult to Jorge, but it was taken as such by James—a reminder of the often inadvertent powers of language.

JT So here's these two thinkers occupying two opposed positions, and their particular way of wording these positions would exert a great influence in the eighties and nineties. Less so now, which is perhaps why it is interesting to discuss them now, and to think about what other words one could use in relation to contemporary art production.

JP I've never really thought about being inside or outside those positions. I'm obviously a little more sympathetic to someone like Dave Hickey, who's a little bit crazy.

JT Both of those figures, in their very different ways, build their arguments around a perception of crisis within the art world.

JP Right. For Buchloh, it's this idea of art being subsumed by entertainment, the work becoming somehow diluted and unable to perform proper cultural criticism.

JT So, that leaves just a few artists who remain able to mount an opposition to that subsuming. And for Buchloh, that opposition has to occur within the institution, because it has to be site-specific, it has to answer to those surrounding conditions...

JP ...And that's because, for him, it *is* an institutional problem. It doesn't really apply to the world outside.

JT There's a fear of the institution of art becoming monopolized, and no longer part of the "public sphere," as he puts it. For Hickey, though, freedom only exists outside the institution, which is always already monopolized, and not by the forces of entertainment or capital, but by other expressly political forces.

JP So that's a classical polemic: the free market versus more institutionally sanctioned forms of consumption. I think both positions are highly problematic and naïve. Buchloh obviously can't speak about the type of institutionalization that he's put forth through this "natural selection" of just a handful of artists who are all extremely successful. These artists are shown by the best galleries, and make a lot of money; they occupy a very forceful position within the institution that doesn't really resonate in a public way.

JT In a way, it is an aristocratic position.

JP The problems that they address were never public problems. They are aesthetic problems.

JT Buchloh does not discuss aesthetics in much detail. That's more Hickey's terrain, but there, the single-minded focus on the aesthetic, the beautiful, and so on, goes in the opposite direction, at times trivializing the potential of art. And a lot of the art that he favors is openly trivial.

JP To some degree that's true, but he supports a number of important artists as well, and it would be interesting to see where he might agree with Buchloh, as a way out or something like that... There's Ed Ruscha for instance, and what's interesting about his work is that it's actually quite systematic. It reflects on aesthetic problems in a subjective, but also ethnographic way.

JT There is a consistent interest in the common, the everyday, the vernacular, which places Ruscha in the populist camp. There is a populist level of access to the work, but there are other levels as well. With someone like Michael Asher, perhaps, there are not so many levels of access. Either you understand what his project is about, or you don't.

JP Asher's work is almost an example of his pedagogy, and it aspires to indoctrination.

JT The Buchloh model is essentially top-down: you have a learned specialist like Asher who reaches out—as you're saying, "pedagogically"—into a very limited public sphere, and indoctrinates the limited public there. Conversely, the Hickey model is more bottom-up inasmuch as the artists he champions, like Ruscha, always have some relation to popular culture, and by way of that culture, to the general public. But they also always have a relation to power, so Hickey never resorts to a simplistic explanation of the aesthetic or beautiful. To him, art is above all a field of contention, and how that actually happens is always to an extent outside the artist's intention. For instance, he discusses the aesthetic function as being akin to advertising; it lends rhetorical thrust to the artist's often marginal or idiosyncratic worldview, but this is not to say that it necessarily succeeds in convincing everyone, and sometimes it does the opposite. At best, it produces a rift between the public, or between a particular public and power.

JP He positivizes the conflict. The aesthetic offers a simplistic entry point to the public, but once you enter in and start to look at the back end of the work, the issues it raises are obviously political, and that's where all the resistance mechanisms of it lie.

JT In that regard, I was again thinking about your notion of the artwork as a kind of portrait of the funders or patrons, but one that is forcefully mediated by the person of the artist, who thereby introduces a secondary portrait of himself. In his *Invisible Dragon*, Hickey discusses a Caravaggio painting of the Madonna (*Madonna of the Rosary*, 1606–07), commissioned by the church to describe a succession of power between the Christ's birth and those who were there to witness it and then those that follow this lineage. These are church representatives, but Caravaggio represents them as lay people, types chosen from his own social circle. He introduces a timely, contingent, problematic element into this holy contract.

JP Hickey goes into the back end of the work, and it's always about the fact that Caravaggio was a crazy guy … And gay! His argument only works because Caravaggio was transgressive, and obviously the church did not feel that his transgression was powerful enough to warrant any resistance to wanting that image.

JT And there are obviously ways to reroute the transgressive element to one's own ends, for purposes of drama, let's say. The priesthood becomes sexy; religion is aestheticized as the object of the artist's desire, and this can then serve as a kind of propaganda.

JP Yes, because it all happens under the radar.

JT The point about aesthetics and advertising is interesting here because one can impute it to early church painting. It mobilizes beauty in support of power. And yet, Hickey suggests that, over time, the particularities of that context fall away, and what we are left with is simply the aesthetic, and that's what then gets exacerbated with someone like Mapplethorpe.

JP The wall labels tell you that he's a fag, so he doesn't just make generally beautiful things; it's beautiful because "I love dicks," or "I love getting fucked in the ass" (*laughs*). And Hickey finds a lot of power in that.

JT He does because these are people who make art out of the things they love, as opposed to the Duchampian model—which is also partly the model of Buchloh—where one deals instead with those things that one has no particular taste for.

JP   So, Hickey will tend to demonize someone like Buchloh because he's functioning like the church to some degree. But then, there's not much about transgression that resonates in the culture anymore. People don't have the same issues about sexuality. It's not the fifties, or sixties...

JT   ... Or even the eighties or nineties, which is when Hickey had his revelation that an artist could still generate, within the space of a museum, a real public debate. In Mapplethorpe's case, it really centered on material questions of government funding, but the way the argument was voiced was ideological. Why should the public have to contend with the work of this "outsider"? And from the other side, it was all about censorship versus free speech.

JP   Both Hickey and Buchloh make a moral argument. So, that was the last gasp, within the art world, for a polemical, issue–based criticism.

JT   To an extent, Hickey brings it to an end. The issue of the nineties, he declares in *Invisible Dragon*, will be beauty. It's an argument that would have a great deal of resonance in the art world. One finds a similar outlook in the writings of Gary Kornblau, David Pagel, Christopher Knight—basically, all the people who wrote for *Art Issues*, where Hickey also published.

JP   It's very American: It's an attempt to make a critical space for the sort of work that was being made in the U.S. in the nineties. The Europeans had a very different take on the period. They take Buchloh's argument and try to play it out by popularizing institutional potential. The socially performative enters the institution with people like Hans Ulrich-Obrist, who operate through similar sorts of methodologies as fashion and commerce, a global scanning for anything with a sliver of social potential. There's an attempt to democratize issues that are actually much more complicated: issues of nationality, of race, of the outsider... The art world becomes internationalized, and it has to find a way to socialize that work. But obviously, at the end of the day, the more different kinds of people and problems and issues you are going to bring into the fold the more interesting it will get for everybody.

14

INSTITUTIONAL CRITIQUE
THE SOCIETY OF ADMINISTRATION
THE COLD WAR
SPECTACLE
FORMAL DETRITUS

Mérida
September 2019

This final series of conversations were all conducted in Mexico over a period of five days at Jorge's house in Mérida. During this time we often spoke while driving: to his studio; to the homes of prospective clients; to the construction site of China Art Objects, the artist's old L.A. gallery, which had followed his southward trail; and finally to *Tecoh*. Throughout my visit, I was struck at how much the area had changed since I last was there in 2002, and also how much Jorge had left his mark on it. The once largely untouched Mérida suddenly seemed like a cosmopolitan hub. Perhaps the clearest sign of his occupation, though, was the fact that at every coffee shop we stopped into the employees all knew him by name: Señor Jorge. The ensuing exchange started inside one of these, a particularly upscale example, indistinguishable from anything one would find in the "arts district" of any major U.S. city. Jorge had asked me if I had seen any interesting shows of late, and I instead brought up some uninteresting ones. I started recording only once we were back in the car.

JP I blame Hans Haacke for all this.

JT What were you saying? "I saw the shadow on the wall ..."

JP ... I mean, the position of all those artists associated with institutional critique is: "We were forecasting this technocratic, administrative clampdown of things." But my position is: "You did not see the shadow on the wall; you did not see into the future. No, you are the fucking shadow on the wall."

JT This is the position they wound up with, by default.

JP They became administrators of their own work. That space that they were used to working with enters this managed condition— basically, to keep at bay its own commercial instrumentalization.

JT   They also perform a service to the institution, in the end, by pointing out its weaknesses.

JP   The work was about telling everybody that the people that are giving us money to make art are slumlords, basically.[51] Of course they're slumlords; they're fucking rich; that's what some rich people do (laughs).

JT   That's maybe where it starts. Again, I'd say that this work performs a service, and it's a twofold service. First, by showing this work, the institution absolves itself. It becomes transparent in a way. It can say, "Yes, I realize that this is the condition we are operating under." So, you put that out there in the attempt to foster a critical dialogue about the system of operation; you absolve yourself from operating in secret. But secondly, I'd say, there's this situation where the artist is recruited as a kind of troubleshooter who starts pointing out the flaws that the administrative apparatus can then begin to fix...

JP   ...Well, the institution can't really point to those things itself; that would be hysterical. You need a seer to manage those kinds of humanistic transgressions (laughs).

JT   Right. But then the position of the artist as seer is in a sense banalized. And the upshot of this, on the other end, is that institutions start to devolve into machines of self-regulation and put on less and less interesting shows.

JP   They stop inquiring into the mechanisms of what they do. They stop dealing with the less manageable contingencies that art produces in favor of those that aren't really that difficult to manage.

51 This relating to Hans Haacke's famously controversial piece from 1971, *Shapolsky et al. Manhattan Real Estate Holdings, A Real-Time Social System, as of May 1, 1971*. Consisting of maps, pedestrian black-and-white photographs of tenement façades, and typewritten sheets detailing the facts related to the value, sale and ownership of the represented properties, this work demonstrated the extent of one corporate entity's control over real estate in the then lower-income neighborhoods of Harlem and the Lower East Side. The work was slated to be included in Haacke's first solo show at the Guggenheim Museum in New York, also in 1971, but met with objections from the director, Thomas Messer, whereupon the whole exhibition was canceled.

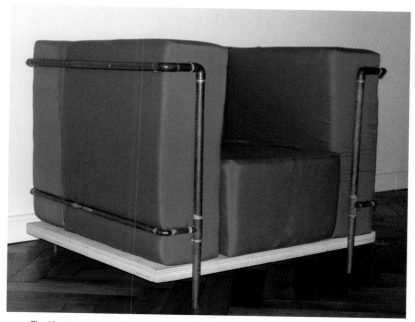

Fig. 16 *Me and My Mum (Blue)*, 1990. Installation view, Museum Dhondt-Dhaenens, Deurle, Belgium.

Fig. 17 *Jorge Pardo*, 2014–15. Installation view neugerriemschneider, Berlin.

Fig. 18 L'Arlatan, 2014–18.

Fig. 19 Reinstallation of Latin American Galleries, Los Angeles County Museum of Art, 2008.

Fig. 20 Display for the Hall of Roman Sculpture, Musée des Augustins, Toulouse, 2014.

JT And you also have the emergence of the administrative curator, someone who doesn't really have a program outside simply managing the situation they're in. So, it becomes all about art world politics—boring.

JP It becomes all about representation. We're starting to sound like right wing antiquota people, but at the end of the day, it's clear that these institutions just aren't agile enough to naturalize their relation to the actual variety of work in the world. So, what they do is calculate the spread and the makeup of what they have to represent, which is fine because this, ultimately, is what institutions are about—they're about the *republic*, and they should reflect the republic to a degree...

JT ...To a degree. So, here I will say that I miss the Cold War. Instead of aligning art with representative government, let's say—this kind of broad-based initiative to include everyone, which in any case is impossible—you had this polarized situation. Two sides face off, but, here and there, also merge. This relates to what we were talking about earlier: during the Cold War there was this covert sharing of cultural or political characteristics. The U.S. had to take on some aspects of Socialism; it couldn't fall behind what was being achieved—civically, let's say, in terms of education, of public projects, what have you—in the East. And vice versa, the East had to take on some of the cultural optimism of the West, the fun aspect. When Khrushchev wanted to visit Disneyland, this was also a fact-finding mission, you know? It's a kind of schizophrenic scenario. I remember, as a kid, going to museums that were run somewhat like Socialist institutions, where art was taken very seriously, where there was clearly an intent to expose and educate, but then I'd be the only person in there. So, this education wasn't being managed, really. And one upshot of this was that curators could fulfill their "vision" of what a museum could, or should, be, and this had nothing to do with answering back to any sort of a public demand, right? This was just culture with a capital C, and it was sort of foisted on you.

JP Exactly.

JT Institutions were kind of irresponsible during this time, but also maybe more interesting. The Cold War reminds me of what's good about dialectics, because if you have these stark oppositions...

JP   ... It's really useful.

JT   Yes, it's useful, but it also produces what I like to call a *zany* culture, and one that's not reducible to a simple either/or formula The sides get mixed up. Back to institutional critique: it comes out of this Cold War period. There's something schizophrenic about inviting an artist into a liberal institution to socialistically take it apart, to literally dismantle the building in some cases. Michael Asher, whom we've talked about a lot, is a classic Cold War artist in that sense, but then there is another side to him that is, I think, very contemporary. The initial perception of him as staying out of the market, resisting it, is today negated by the fact that the market seems to have turned Asheresque. His work feeds directly into our new economic standard: the economy of attention and experience, of immaterial goods.

JP   Michael Asher's *completely* zany (*laughs*). Just think about it, he says, "I'm going to use these kinds of, what, transparency triggers, and I'm going to use them as art." And they're weird; that's what's interesting about them. They produce all this formal detritus. And then he says, "I'm going to make sure that this detritus can't be instrumentalized as commerce," which is basically impossible.

JT   One thing that's become apparent to me, while looking at the pictures from his famous 1974 show at Claire Copley Gallery, where he took out the wall separating the front viewing space from the business space in back, is how a move like that has become pretty much the commercial standard. I'm thinking about how, in almost every restaurant today, the kitchen is exposed. It used to be sealed off from the view of the guests for reasons of propriety, or maybe more sinister reasons, but it turns out that seeing your food being cooked is a bonus. It adds to the experience.

JP   This work was so easily rerouted into capitalism. That's what makes it zany: it doesn't work.

JT   Those kitchens *do* work, though.

JP   *They* work, but his mechanisms of exposing these things don't. You know, instead of giving you a piece of art, an object in a room, his object in a room is this idea that there's a dichotomy between the back, which is commerce, and the front, which is culture. That doesn't work because we are all implicated within a bigger system. So now you get open kitchens, open studios ...

JT   What if someone came to the Claire Copley show and found no political message in there, and just became interested in what this person does in the back of the gallery? This aspect of the piece is rarely considered: that the gallerist is in a way forced to put on a show. Her everyday work is turned into a performance; it's theatricalized.

JP   You'd have to be really naïve to think that you're seeing how the gallery really works. Because the first thing that I would notice— let's say, if I knew nothing about art—is that the artist has forced the person in back to be the object of the show, and there's an *awkwardness*, always, associated with this. Whether there's enthusiasm on their part or whether they're going, "That fucking Michael Asher, he's now making me talk to these people when it was so nice just to do the books," there's always going to be awkwardness. That's the first thing I would see; I would actually reduce it to the most aggressive gesture of wanting to show me this.

JT   I'm with you. It's not that you are revealing what was once hidden, but that you're turning something banal into a spectacle.

JP   Well, it's not banal to the gallerist. But I'm always more interested in things like what the fuck is the exhibition, you know? What does it take to put together the exhibition? What is the artist puppetmastering here? To think that you might actually learn something about the quotidian through this move is naïve.

JT   I also like to think about what happens to moves like this over time, or what they engender. Back to the restaurant, it turns out that seeing your food being prepared adds a kind of drama to the meal. This is one upshot of Asher's project. But then something else also happens, and this goes back to what we were talking about earlier: you don't expose the secret but rather show that there is nothing secret going on here. This is the administrative part. You're allowed to say, "We run a clean kitchen. You should not be nervous about anything that comes out of it." What you were saying about Hans Haacke is related to this, because you're giving the object of your critique the possibility to absolve itself of the problem.

JP Right. But it is also a totally sadistic move, and it becomes even more dark with people like Christopher Williams or Stephen Prina, who were both students of Asher. These are artists I find very interesting and who, by the way, were part of my formation. They're smart enough to smell the commerce in those kinds of conceptual maneuvers, in everything that is idiosyncratic and strange about them. And so they start to legislate that potential by attributing all these rules and regulations on where their work begins and ends. They say, "Look, if you do this, the work is no longer mine, or if you do that, it is no longer a work." They create these boundaries around what exactly the work is. These are some of the most prescriptive artists that I've ever met. Everything down to the fabrication of the work is potential fodder for what it draws in as its subject: you know, where it was made, how it was made, how long it took ... What are the obvious associations or the not so obvious associations?—all of this is managed somehow. This is less and less true of Prina now, but more and more so of Williams, who is maybe a more effective commercial instrument (*laughs*). Because one of the things that you do when you so forcefully limit how you can and cannot show the work, or what's to be seen or not seen in it, is that you rarify it.

JT They *applied* the lesson of Michael Asher ...

JP They went to CalArts and, like I always say, CalArts was a career college, basically a finishing school. What you learn there is basically how to sell art, and these guys were smart enough to know that. You know, they understood that they could take Michael Asher and instrumentalize the shit out of him, even instrumentalize the things that he put in place that made it impossible to sell his work, to turn even that into valuable product.

JT Mostly what you're talking about is this "formal detritus," as you put it. They seized on the aesthetic fallout of Asher's project, which you do as well.

JP With Asher, you end up with this kind of clean-core proposition that doesn't really work. But all around it, this detritus is produced, and it's sort of unmanageable, and that's what *I* like about his work. I like all the things about it that *he* doesn't like. I like its failed aspect, the tragic side of institutional critique, the drama of it, you know? I read it almost like Russian literature.

JT   Right. So, here's what I'm thinking: in Asher's piece for Claire Copley, we are presented with, ostensibly, the gallery as the work, and it's considered generically as just a gallery like any other. But by the time we get to Prina and Williams, we start to move toward the specifics.

JP   They begin to appropriate the specifics…

JT   …Everything that was not accounted for in Asher's own rhetoric.

JP   Well, with Asher you have this sort of strict rhetoric. It's like going into K-Mart and someone says, "Look at these shoes! They're fantastic! But you can't buy them…" That's crazy, and Prina and Williams recognized that there was an entertainment value in that.

JT   Well, the fact that you can go to a store and not buy anything is today not necessarily such a bad thing. The understanding of how commodities operate has been projected way beyond the cash register. This is not the end of the economic exchange. In fact, you could say that the economy increasingly works to promote endless-ness: you subscribe to products rather than buy them outright.

JP   It's part of brand building and, yes, that is the detritus.

JT   So, I've been rereading our earliest conversations, and this goes back to the idea that in order to understand anything in art you have to consider its history, to, again, connect the dots between one work and the next. I think that Asher was so adamant about this. His caravan project for Münster, for instance, has to be understood in its unfolding over these ten year periods.[52] So, we have to keep returning to its origins, but then also, as Adorno says, "art is what it has become," and this often is something very different from what any artist intended.

JP   What I find most interesting—and also most tragic—in his work is this need to control all the specifications. So, Asher has to have this very specific camping trailer for the first show, and then after ten years pass, he has to have exactly the same one, and they have a really hard time finding it. Of course, the first thing I think of is what does it mean that it has to be exactly the same? You know, what would happen if it were close to, but not the same? Would it be uncanny? Would it diminish the earnestness of it? Would it work like a painting that had somehow been damaged? This need to control the situation, does it make it work better? Or is it because he's a sadomasochist? These thoughts are also part of the formal detritus of the work, but when you look at this detritus, you don't just say, "Well, that's interesting," and leave it at that. You say, "What the fuck does that produce?"

JT Yes, so the generation that follows seizes on this, on the psychological tone, maybe, of these operations.

JP And then Asher was also obsessed with ephemera, with these objects that stand in for the ephemeral—or, at least, that's one way of putting it. He really had to make sure that these very elaborate cards and invitations were sent out, and that's something that could be taken away at the end of the show. But it was always made clear that this was ephemera, like the ticket you keep after a concert, so that there could never be any confusion between this thing and the work itself. What's important is to be at the show—that's the takeaway.

52 In 1977, Michael Asher participated in the first iteration of Skulptur Projecte Münster, an exhibition organized by Kaspar König that was held in the Westfälisches Landesmuseum für Kunst und Kulturgeschichte and various locations across the city. The following description of Asher's contribution is sourced from the Skulptur Projekte archives: "He (Asher) made a work for Münster, which consisted of a rented Hymer-Eriba Familia camping trailer. Every Monday, while the museum was closed to the public, over the course of the nineteen-week exhibition the trailer was moved to another part of the city. It was therefore relocated nineteen times to nineteen different positions in and around Münster, a number intentionally corresponding to the timeframe of the exhibition. Asher strategically sited the caravan so it gradually radiated further away from the governing center of the exhibition, the museum … At each site, the trailer was parked and remained locked. Its curtains were pulled closed without any indication the object was art. The locations where Asher decided to situate the trailer were everyday spots, ranging from parallel parking spaces on the street in front of apartment buildings, offices, and shops, to light-industrial sites, parks, and the banks of a canal. As the weeks of the exhibition came to a close, the object, too was drawn back incrementally closer to the museum. Available at the museum's front desk, a regularly updated handout, considered an essential part of the work, provided information of the whereabouts of the caravan and set museum visitors out of the institution and into the city streets of Münster to find the trailer." Skulptur Projekte Münster takes place every ten years, and Asher is the only artist who has participated in it on four consecutive occasions, right up until his death in 2012. Each time, the attempt was made to show exactly the same trailer in the same locations.

JT   But then what happens with the artists that follow in the wake of Asher is that they begin to devote more and more attention to the ephemera as something that is no longer peripheral to the project.

JP   The ephemera is centralized. It becomes an object, an object of exchange.

JT   That's another service to the current economy that Asher might have performed. The value of the ephemeral has moved beyond art. So many goods today are infused with this kind of existential content...

JP   ... Things that allow you to say, "I was there." It's how you build a cult: you give the people ephemera.

15

POP ART
RADICAL REDUCTION
BOHEMIA AND SOCIETY
THE TIMELY AND
THE UNTIMELY
VULGARITY

Mérida
September 2019

That we start this next conversation once more on the subject of Michael Asher might give the impression that we are somehow obsessed with this artist, which is not entirely untrue. But if we keep returning to familiar themes, it is also because I have been rereading all of our transcripts from start to finish and want to get back to certain points perhaps too quickly left off. In other words, the effect of a very slowly turning feedback loop should be factored in. From Asher, we quickly turn to Andy Warhol, another figure who has been mentioned before, and one with whom Jorge obviously feels a certain kinship. As noted, he had delivered a lecture on Warhol at Dia in 2002, and, in what follows, we discuss Jorge's relation to this artist's position on Pop art, and in particular to the work that so many critics found hard to support.

JT   Asher seems like such a fitting contemporary model for the corpo-
       rate class.

JP   Just think of Asher as someone who's making an advertising plat-
       form. It's incredibly effective.

JT   I recently saw a billboard imprinted with the words, "This space
       intentionally left blank." It catches your attention and holds it.
       There is an implied critique of advertising, but what it actually
       produces is curiosity. You want to know what comes next, which in
       a way is the punchline: the product. So, these critical models have
       been successfully infused into corporate culture. But then, on the
       other side of Asher, whose work was basically appropriated by
       market forces, there's someone like Andy Warhol, who comman-
       deers those forces. You've spoken about Warhol; he's an important
       figure for you, obviously.

JP   My Warhol lecture at Dia had to do with flatness, the idea that
       there was just one type of painting that could cover every type of
       subject. Warhol, more than anybody else, chose such a "fuck you"

way to paint that you always have to respond to this distance. And then it's surrounded by all these funny aberrations, like the magazine [*Interview*] or the video portraits [*Screen Tests*, 1964–66] ...

JT Well, there's all the work that everybody loves that reflects on society, and then there's the work that is just part of society, that's symptomatic of being social. And in the portraits also there's a division between the portraits of the people in the Factory, who have a bohemian relation to society, and then the other portraits where Warhol presents himself as a kind of court painter for the wealthy and popular.

JP Yes, he basically designed a way to be a court painter in the present, and to sort of spew out everything that is disgusting about representing these people, while also loving them at the same time. Warhol was a dirty man; it's a dirty project.

JT There's works where you can gauge a distance from the subject and then works where there is no distance at all. And Warhol doesn't really pull the self-reflexive Velazquez move of flipping the perspective around ...

JP ... He has no interest in picture-making; that's what's interesting about him.

JT But how do you speak about that? There is still a kind of Warholian gesture ... Artists had emptied out paintings before—I mean, *fully* emptied them out. I'm thinking here of something like [Robert] Rauschenberg's *White Paintings*, for instance.

JP But they're not really empty. They're actually generous in the process of emptying out. Like, there's something *spectacular* in the fact that they're white. They have no image, but the difference with Warhol is that the image *sucks*.

JT That's a different kind of flatness.

JP The image is ridiculous; it responds to such a minimum requirement to be an image. And that, in the end, is much more *brutal* than any white painting.

JT Rauschenberg's paintings can still serve as a kind of Zen platform.

JP Warhol's paintings are embalmed; they're *dead*.

JT There's something in them of the deflation we had talked about earlier in regard to Manet.

JP Yes, but Warhol is different. Because Manet is really activating the painting, every part of the painting, and he is very traditional in that sense. You could even say that about the *White Paintings*. But Warhol is not that. It's like, "Find a picture of Jackie, start up the printing machine, OK, we got it." That's how it works.

JT This is a portrait of someone we recognize; Jackie O. means something in America; the public has a certain way of identifying with her, maybe tragically. And then—not in spite of that, but precisely because of that—there's a deliberate attempt to deflate any significance the picture might carry.

JP Or to deflate the correlation between the significance of the image and the significance of its production. That is why it's embalmed. Because artists are generally in the business of putting life into gestures, and Warhol doesn't do that. Making a Warhol is a ridiculously detached enterprise: like, there's an outline, there's some filler, there's maybe a couple of colors, and that's it! There's no investigation of any of it being in the right or the wrong place; it's usually centralized. There's no attempt to activate the square; it doesn't matter. It's very tragic work for people who are invested in Manet-type painting, which is all about reanimating the process of painting every time it comes up.

JT Last night, were looking at that Maximilian painting [Édouard Manet, *The Execution of Emperor Maximilian*, 1868–69] and commenting about the somewhat bored or distracted expressions of the onlookers peering over the wall at the killing. So, the artist sets up an expectation—this is history painting; it depicts a historically significant scene—but then he deflates this expectation in his treatment of it. Manet is proto-Pop art in this sense. It's in this dispassionate way of looking at something intense, and I think that this is in Warhol's Jackie portrait as well. Something is set up or promised, and then something else is delivered.

JP   But Warhol does even less. Because everything had already been resolved way before the Jackie painting; formally, it's set. What we want to find in the Warhol is, first of all, a Warhol. It's like a LeRoy Neiman in that sense.

JT   Well, that's why you could say that the later work—the work many people label schlock—is actually more daring. Because the further away you get from the early Warhol, where there still is a connection to bohemianism and to the New York demimonde, and the closer you get to the later Warhol with its more mainstream relation to society, there is the real danger of finding oneself wholly outside of art. This has to do with the expectation that artists look at things from a different perspective, or that they remain to some extent social outcasts. It's the insider perspective of the later Warhol that's really distressing to some viewers, and it becomes more distressing as it becomes blander.

JP   I don't really see much difference between Warhol's early and late work. To me it's all on a kind of zipper, just one thing after the other. That's what's interesting about him: *Interview* is the same as Jackie is the same as Coke. These are just images sourced from popular culture, you know? Maybe as he becomes more invested in fashion, this just becomes more direct. Even the *Screen Tests* he worked on have the same qualities, because you're basically just getting a headshot of someone. I read Warhol as someone who's so consistently flat that it's almost impossible for him to make a move that is more or less artlike than anything else.

JT   Still, with the *Screen Tests*, there is the notion that you're giving your public a view into a side of life that they're not familiar with. It's the world of these "superstars" that were part of his Factory menagerie, and these aren't real superstars; they're drag queens and speed freaks. So, there he's still operating on the model of the artist as outsider who gives you a glimpse into another world, whereas with the Jackie image, that relates to a real superstar, someone we all know, a known quantity. I still think there's a kind of progression described there from the margins toward the center of society.

JP   I never thought of Warhol as an outsider. I mean, he started as an illustrator; so he was always on the inside, to a degree. In the end, he just gets a much larger platform—that's about it.

JT   Yeah, this mention of illustration is important. You brought up LeRoy Neiman, who is such an insider that he's totally outside of art. I mean, we don't tend to think of Neiman as someone who's part of our art world. There's a big difference between Pop art and truly popular art in this sense. But Warhol obviously wanted to ride that line. That he actually staged a two-person show with LeRoy Neiman obviously speaks to this point.[53]

JP   Yeah. Warhol is interesting because he's one degree of separation away from Neiman. So, what happens when you do a show like that is that you produce an optic through which to look at popular culture, whereas Neiman, I'd say, is indifferent to that. There's a very strange kind of reflexivity involved.

JT   Well, on the one hand, it's shocking, because he's mixing art with nonart. But on the other hand, Warhol is also saying, "This is also where I come from; we're not so dissimilar."

JP   Yeah, or maybe he just thought LeRoy Neiman was fabulous because he was *so* popular (*laughs*). Nobody knows what to do, really, with the reflexive mechanism of Warhol because he was such a master at distancing himself from it.

JT   Right. I wonder what you think about Pop art in general, or if there is any part of your own practice that you would label Pop?

JP   Well, I'm not so interested in general in Pop art, but what I am interested in is its indifference to the referent. It's always assumed that in Pop art the referent is going to be meaningful because it exists in quotidian life, but as a deep investigation of values, you know, I've never taken that seriously. What I like about Pop art is that it allows you to be indifferent about how you appropriate things.

JT   Pop art is not only about popularity, but also, I'd say, about timeliness, about responding to what is new.

JP   In order for Pop art to be popular, the referent has to have some critical mass, right? It has to already be mediated to some extent,

53 *LeRoy Neiman, Andy Warhol: An Exhibition of Sports Paintings* was held at the Institute of Contemporary Art in Los Angeles in 1981.

and through that mediation you can bring in content that's already kind of set up for you. And that's why I think it's interesting: it allows you to access a loaded readymade referent. But that's also why it's not interesting: it's not complex. You have a very hard time trying to shake out any more from it than that.

JT   We've talked about duration in the past, but not so much about time. I'm thinking that in order to play with duration, as you like to do, you also have to consider the temporal context within which it unfolds—that is, the timeliness or untimeliness of the work, how it reverberates with current affairs and with the so-called state of the art.

JP   I try always to be in the present. Even when I refer to something in the past, I'll always incorporate something of the present, but this is a very deadpan operation.

JT   One place that this idea of timeliness could come in is in your embrace of technology.

JP   Well, what I don't want to happen is for the use of technology to be so overbearing that it becomes spectacle. I'm more interested in normalizing these conditions of technology.

JT   Maybe more interesting would be to apply this question of timeliness to that of style. For instance, there might be colors that are of the moment, that have an up-to-the-minute kind of currency, versus colors that are passé. Architecture, furniture, décor, etc.—these are all things that carry a particular time signature. Is this something that you attend to at all in your work?

JP   I've never consciously brought in a color system from a particular period. You have to make references that are much more open than that. I mean, color, itself, is much more open than that. Whenever I make color systems, I always pretend that they're happening right now.

JT   You pretend that they're happening right now... I'm wondering if some of the choices you make also have to do with what you've talked about—and you've stressed its importance—as the negotiation with the client?

JP   Well, sometimes they do and sometimes they don't. I've always tried to convolute it to some degree. I'll give you an example: I'm doing a box for Cuervo—you know, for their fancy tequila—and I gave them a series of colors, and the owner said that he'd really like for *this* color to be in there, and I got back to him and I said, "That's great, let's collaborate. Now my color is the color you've picked!" And there's a kind of consciousness that comes through of looking at the ridiculousness, the arbitrariness of that.

JT   So, here's where you could be taking something from Warhol. You said that the first thing that you look for in a Warhol is a Warhol, which on the one hand is a kind of tautology, or an operation that points to a tautological structure. But, from the perspective of a lay audience, what is also being looked for is a kind of self-portrait. Warhol's paintings are popular because they reflect an upward climb on Warhol's part. In other words, there's a kind of story behind them, an autobiography, and it moves between bohemia and society. At some point he's making portraits not only of society, but with society.

JP   You have to remember, though, that bohemia is part of society. There is no bohemia without society. It's a dialectic; they are two sides of the same coin.

JT   Well, that's true, and it's interesting, but maybe we can say that artists often try to juggle these two sides of life. And they try to render the discrepancies between them visible, legible to the audience. With Warhol, this feeds into a kind of narrative that the audience finds compelling, and this narrative is being written as much by Warhol as his clients. So, we have these films starring the people that work for him, the "superstars," and then we come to Jackie: it's a kind of aspirational American story. Warhol works his way up the ranks, while also opening up a channel for a kind of downward mobility on the part of those that he paints.

JP   What stands out with Warhol is the *flagrant* way he throws himself into that. It's like, anyone can work, this work can be made about anyone, as long as they have any kind of public profile. The process is flagrantly undiscriminating; that's what I think scares people. I don't know if this has to do with client relations... It's more in the way that he constructs the subject with this kind of extreme indifference. Anyone can be the subject of this work; they can come from so many different places; they can *pay* to be the subject, you know what I mean? It's kind of horrifying and beautiful at the same time.

JT   Would you say that there is any place for the word "vulgarity" in a description of Warhol?

JP   No, just like there's no vulgarity in the bohemian. The bohemian is a highly stratified social entity. Bohemia is a well-understood roadway into society. There's nothing in Warhol that gets rich people to do what they don't want to do.

JT   Well, vulgarity does have a pejorative ring, but it also means simply the common, the everyday. And here I'd like to turn this conversation back to you, because clearly you have an investment in Warhol and maybe are also taking a cue from him. I'm thinking that it might have to do with the way that you juggle a kind of elite notion of taste with something maybe baser. A good example would be the Le Corbusier sofa, which you remade out of plumbing fixtures (*Me and My Mum (Blue)*, 1990) (fig. 16). There's some bathroom humor in there.

JP   Well, it's a ridiculous piece. You're making something that's highly refined, and you're making it out of materials that normally are hidden in the wall. And on top of that, your mother gets used as a material in the work, which is even more debasing.

JT   Materials hidden in the wall, but more specifically materials that could carry some kind of scatological content. It makes me relate the Corbusier to a toilet seat. And then with the addition of your mother, there's a sly nod to toilet training, maybe?

JP   Yeah. Everything is in service to this relationship that's basically in the business of producing humor. We try to make things where describing them or explaining them hopefully reaches clarity and absurdity at the same time. As an aside, I did grow up in one of those seats from the sixties that had a toilet in it, so you would eat and shit at the same time (*laughs*).

JT   I guess I'm going on about this because Warhol also made that series of paintings with piss. (*Piss Paintings* and *Oxidation Paintings*, 1977–78)

JP I think that the operative principle of that work falls into exactly what I was describing about bohemia: even when you pee, you don't lose your social standing. When someone makes piss paintings, they're having a good time thinking about them because it's ridiculous, and it's even more ridiculous that they could be construed as refined. But then there's also an ordinariness to them. For me, it's not so interesting to focus on the scatological aspect; what is interesting is how these motions are muted in relation to exhibition characteristics. Everything comes clean in the gallery. You can yell, you can climb the walls like Matthew Barney, you can stick an icicle up your ass, blah, blah, blah—it all comes clean in the white cube.

JT You've returned to this theme. I recently saw some reproductions of a show where you constructed a bathroom right in the middle of the gallery.

JP That was at neugerriemschneider (*Jorge Pardo*, November 15, 2014–January 24, 2015.) (fig. 17) There were two of them actually, and you could use them, if you liked—they work. I was thinking of them as something someone might want to stick in their house somewhere. Everybody always needs an extra bathroom, you know? And these could work as an outdoor sculpture or an indoor sculpture. I was also interested in working all these inherent sculptural problems through them. Like, if you start to play out the formalities, I thought it was interesting that the plinth for a sculpture like that is the sewer system. I was thinking about how an object like that *fits* into an exhibition context. You know, how does this object extend and deform the supposed neutrality that's put into place in a gallery for an object to be properly seen?

JT This goes back to Duchamp, who was also a hero of Warhol's, incidentally.

JP Well, but my works are also performative. You've got to remember that Duchamp's urinal didn't work.

JT You've mentioned before that you want to "constipate" the viewer's ability to read the work, or to arrive at a totalized reading. These bathrooms are funny in relation to that because they presuppose, or even welcome, an unconstipated viewer. If one were to actually use the sculpture, would this complete it, do you think? Inasmuch as plumbing is the plinth for this work, the toilet is also a pedestal for whoever sits on it.

JP   The person becomes more like a part of the landscape of the bathroom because this thing is highly aestheticized. The structure works as a frame for the person who simply becomes part of the décor of the bathroom. It's simply a way of flipping all this stuff around. You know, who is the subject and what is the object? It's a very strange sculptural machine, and what's important about how it works is that it is *involuntary*.

16

PUBLIC AND PRIVATE ART
CLIENT AND/OR PATRON RELATIONS
SITE-SPECIFICITY

Mérida
September 2019

The first part of this conversation was recorded on-site at *Tecoh*, which is located near the town of Izamal, about an hour's drive outside Mérida. We talked while touring its expansive grounds, passing from one building to the next, first the large meeting halls, communal dining rooms, kitchens and bars and finally a series of intimate palapas, appointed for private use, each one color-coded with a different arrangement of bright tiles. Apart from the man who opened the gate and two maintenance employees seen from a distance, it was deserted—a not untypical state of affairs, Jorge informed me. The effect was distinctly haunting, and the riotous exuberance of Jorge's design did nothing to mitigate this—quite the contrary. Though it was not recorded, I recall suggesting that he should direct a remake of *Last Year at Marienbad* in this setting, to which he replied something to the effect of, "Why bother, since it is already happening anyway?" Interestingly, there was not the slightest trace of disappointment in his voice. We continued talking on the drive back to Mérida, turning our attention from *Tecoh* to *L'Arlatan*, Jorge's most recent large-scale project, a hotel and artist residency in Arles, which had opened its doors in 2018.

JT   The last time we talked about the *Tecoh* project, you were still considering what its possible usage might be. So now I'm wondering what actually happened here?

JP   Nothing.

JT   Not a thing?

JP   This is a place that's like an artwork in a museum, except it's in a jungle. It's always maintained.

JT But people do stay here.

JP Not very often; maybe six or seven times a year. The owners invite their friends and colleagues to stay here, but I'd say ninety-nine percent of the time the space is empty.

JT Well then, it's less like a work in a museum than something like an earthwork. Like Heizer's *Double Negative* or Smithson's *Spiral Jetty*, the remoteness of the location and the approach to it is part of the experience.

JP Yeah, absolutely.

JT So, those two projects wound up on opposed ends of a commitment to entropy, which was the big issue of the sixties. Heizer opted to have his work maintained, whereas Smithson, at least nominally, always wanted to let it go. I wonder if your project has anything to do with entropy?

JP Not really. It's not mine. I sold it; it's a commercial project. But all those earthwork guys left the cities and went out into nature because they thought it was more pure, and I'm more interested in using nature as a kind of theatrical setup, not necessarily because of the experiential authenticity it might promote. I'm interested in using nature because of its *artifice*.

JT Like this bird you pointed out to me, which grooms itself to carefully displace those two blue feathers on its tail.[54] This bird is maybe an instance in nature where you might observe an impulse that serves no other purpose than aesthetic splendor.

JP (*Laughing*) It wants to propagate!

JT Which is inarguably a function...

JP ...But it's about as close as you're going to get, in birds, to the pleasure principle.

54 This bird is the Momoto cejiazul. It is generally accepted that its tail feathers are displaced in the course of its flight as opposed to its grooming habits. However, the latter explanation survives in Mayan folklore, and is arguably more compelling than the scientific one.

JT Well, if getting laid is the aesthetic payoff for the birds, what would you say is the equivalent here?

JP Here? I think you come in and you're hit with this sort of perverse aesthetic pleasure that you have a hard time negotiating because you always have to contend with this artistic notion of nature.

JT At the same time, everything in it has a prescribed function: this is a meeting room, this is bedroom, this is a bathroom—we know what to do with these rooms.

JP Sure. It carries all the functions of any type of shelter or habitat. But what's interesting about it is that it doesn't really have a program, and this goes back to the idea of the folly, because everything here that's not being used is just being consumed as visuality. I think it's interesting that it's empty; I'm *still* wondering, "What the fuck is it?" I mean, a folly is usually just a structure in a garden, something that takes you from here to there, but somehow also mitigates the organizing principle of the garden. And you could say the same about this, except that this is strange because the folly takes the shape of a house that's not really being used for any concrete purpose. So, it's a perversion of a folly.

JT The concert hall that Fitzcarraldo wanted to build in the Amazon might be a folly of this kind.[55] It has an ostensible purpose, but it can't be realized because it's too far out, literally.

JP That's different. Fitzcarraldo wanted to bring culture to the jungle. So, you might be surprised that there's an opera house in the jungle, but you won't be confused. He's on a kind of hysterical mission, this idea that something so large, so human, has to go to a place where it isn't now. What I did here [in *Tecoh*] is not that. This area is full of haciendas. The context of this is very similar to all the hotels that exist in the region, except that this isn't a hotel.

55 A reference to Werner Herzog's 1982 film *Fitzcarraldo*. The narrative concerns an Irish adventurer, played by Klaus Kinski, who becomes involved in the Peruvian rubber trade in the hopes of building an opera house in the port city of Iquitos. His plan largely fails, and yet, in the end, he does manage to stage a magisterial performance from the deck of his ship. In the closing scene of the film, the residents of Iquitos— a mixture of Indigenous peoples and colonists—gather on the shore to witness the event.

JT I wasn't expecting this haunted aspect of the place. I suppose this is simply what happens as a result of it being completely empty, with only these caretakers sort of wafting about. Still, it's now doubly empty because it was built around an abandoned factory, and now seems even more abandoned.

JP Again, I think that emptiness, that ghoulishness is a function of it lasting without a program. I had no idea of how long it would be there without getting used much. It's been six or seven years, and the place is perfect ... and it's in the middle of the jungle! We're the only ones there, walking around what is essentially a modern ruin.

JT The space is well maintained, but you're fully aware that the process of natural erosion is always going on there, that the entire construction could so easily be reclaimed by its environment. It would seem that this is part of the drama of it.

JP Yeah, I agree, it's a very opulent structure in this very vulnerable place. The only thing that keeps it there, and that kind of suspends that sense of drama you're talking about, is that it's perfectly kept up. But in another sense, I've always thought of it as a model for how all art works. You know, there are very few old pictures that still have the original paint, the original colors, on them.

JT Here and there, you invite and highlight these natural processes— for instance, in the decision to affix henequen netting to the exterior concrete walls of some of these buildings. Plants climb up this surface as it is rotting away.

JP It invites mold, and it turns that mold into a surface finish.

JT I wonder if you could say anything about landscaping in general, or as a kind of quasi-architectural practice, since it is actually a big part of the work you do.

JP I mean, I don't try to do too many flip-flops with that; it's just straightforward spacemaking.

JT But what about in terms of process? You've worked with Ivette [Soler], and I remember her describing the planting she did for *4166 Sea View Lane* as excessive, and even as kind of monstrous. You were looking at plants that were outside the canon of what one might find in Monet's garden at Giverny, for instance.

JP   Yeah. So, when I do gardens, I do try to make them feel, and literally be, out of scale. Most landscaping is generally in support of the architecture, whereas I'm more interested in it butting up against the architecture so closely that it obscures it in some way. I'm interested in a landscape that might eat the building, or have that kind of fantastical quality to it.

JT   Your new project in Arles (fig. 18), though, is not a folly at all; it's a hotel, plain and simple.[56]

JP   It rides the line between a boutique hotel and something stranger, because it employs a lot of eccentric formal moves— like, it has a six-thousand-square-meter floor of tiles that change, the colors and patterns change every square meter. Six thousand square meters is like … an acre and a half.

JT   It's like the main square of a small town.

JP   Yeah. We made the tiles right here in the Yucatán. I found this dilapidated ceramic factory and we kind of brought it back to life with this project in the hopes that they could keep it running, but they were too lame.

JT   What exactly was the brief of this project?

56 L'Arlatan is a hotel and artist residency designed by Pardo, working closely with the project's founder, the pharmaceutical heiress, art collector, and philanthropist Maja Hoffman, in Arles, France. It is built around the remains of a Roman basilica, which was converted, in the fifteenth century, into a palace for the Counts of Arlatan de Beaumont, and thereafter has been trafficked with in all sorts of ways throughout the years. The finished building boasts forty-one guest rooms in total as well as a variety of communal spaces. Most of the furniture and décor in it was designed and constructed by Pardo, working with a twenty-six-person team in his studio in Mérida. Alongside the expansive Luma Arles art center, launched by Hoffman in 2014, with a soon to be completed Frank Gehry tower as its anchor, the hotel is part of a bid to transform Arles into an international cultural hub. L'Arlatan, which took some four years to complete, was unveiled to the public in the fall of 2018.

JP The brief? Maja Hoffman called me and said, "I bought a hotel for you to work on," and that was it. She asked me, "What do you want to do?" And I said, "Let's find out." We didn't know how many rooms we would have—nothing—until we worked through it. Everything changed in that place. We did all the architecture for it: we did all the room divisions, how the whole thing flows, what historical parts got left in, what was taken out. We were limited in terms of what could be torn down because that place is so historically charged, but in general Maja is smart enough to realize that this project would be much more interesting if it was left open.

JT So, this again comes back to the client relation as a formative element in the work.

JP Well, you have to remember that Maja is a patron and not a client—there's a significant difference.

JT I recall you telling me once, a long time ago, that you had developed a kind of strategy for dealing with clients, or patrons. Here's how I interpreted this: instead of coming to the table with a fully formed plan, which then, in the course of negotiation, is always altered, and often in a way that one might experience with disappointment, you start with something very vague. You give the client a great deal of leeway to express their desire, but then, on the basis of that, you give yourself the opportunity to have the last word. You say something like, "OK, we'll do it your way, but we'll do it like *this*." So, there is never that perception that the work has been somehow derailed. It's maybe a way of protecting oneself?

JP In *L'Arlatan*, like in *Tecoh*, there was a processional model of development. I mean, we knew that it was going to be a hotel, and we knew that there were certain sorts of legal matters associated with that, but in general we made decisions as we went along, decisions that normally would have been made much earlier on. And that's because I don't have any respect for the original architectural impulse. I don't usually come into a project with ideas; I come in without ideas. So, it's not so much about saving myself; I just never want this to be an ideological operation from the get-go. I'm interested in implanting myself in a corrupt situation from the get-go. It's about setting up a kind of hopeful resistance to any ideological framework.

JT How would you characterize your relationship to site in this case? Hotels often respond to their sites in a manner that might be described as themed—the themed architecture of "scripted space," as Norman Klein puts it.[57] But if *L'Arlatan* is to be considered as both a hotel and a work of art then maybe it is more beholden to a logic of site-specificity. I'd say that there is a difference between that and thematic construction.

JP The site-specificity aspect was set up for me from the beginning, because it's a listed historical building. But part of the building is a Roman church that's probably two thousand years old, and another part of it was built in the eighties. So, historically, it was, and is, a clusterfuck. It's very difficult to extract any kind of unifying theme from that. But that, to me, is fantastic. Any kind of decision you make becomes reflexive almost by default.

JT What's an example of a decision that responds to this "clusterfuck" condition?

JP Oh God, there's so many examples, because there were so many issues. In the process, we came across so many things that couldn't be touched: painted ceilings that couldn't be taken down, or Roman columns hidden behind walls. That went on a year into the process of demolition and construction. You know, in France they have the "Patrimoine de France," and so you have to have an official architectural historian onboard, and they're all about maintaining and restoring, whereas for me it's always about what can I fuck with? And these people point that out too: they decide what you don't have to restore. They're useful.

JT It's useful to have limits, to know just what you can and can't do.

JP Yes, so, Maja has so many projects down there that she always has some kind of issue with these people. She feels that she's essentially supporting that town and that area, and they can be

---

57 On "scripted space," see Norman Klein, *The Vatican to Vegas: A History of Special Effects* (New York: The New Press, 2004), 2: "... from 1550 to the present ... These spaces were set up to provide only the fragrance of desire, for political or financial profit. But most of all, they were set up to release a 'marvel,' a briefly eloquent stupefaction. Its effect could be a trifle bawdy, yet safe enough for a church ...."

very persnickety with her—it's like they're getting in her way. But, in general, I always assumed that I was going to defer to them because that's their job, you know? For me, the negotiation process is fun. It's always about what can happen through the process. I tend always to act passively and collect contingencies.

JT In so many of the recent projects you've worked on—and here I'm thinking of *Tecoh* and *L'Arlatan*, as well as your display design for the pre-Columbian wing of LACMA (fig. 19)[58] and, more recently the Musée des Augustins in Toulouse (fig. 20)[59]—you're contending with artifacts, things that are historically precious.

JP Yeah, but I would never want for there to be some clever faux researched–based history motion within it. I mean, it always has to be understood that I'm functioning as a nonexpert in these objects that I'm actually just fucking with. I don't want to be religiously responsible for them. I don't think the goody-goody stuff is good for you.

JT Nevertheless, this architectural historian you were working with probably taught you a thing or two?

JP He was very helpful in shaping the project as it was happening. His various negations, his limiting or opening up the possibilities—I just think of that as constructing another optic. And, yes, there's information in it.

58 Pardo's redesign of the fourth floor of the Art of the Ancient Americas building at LACMA was completed in the summer of 2008. Although he worked closely with the institution's senior curator of pre-Columbian art, the late Virginia Fields, the result vigorously counters the sort of bleached and discreet exhibition protocols normally applied to collections of this sort. This begins with the color-coding of the rooms along a shifting spectrum that reflects the hues of the objects displayed and the regions they are drawn from, but without being beholden to them in any kind of strict sense. This treatment, with all its improvisational leeway, might be described as "painterly," just as the treatment of the display structures—plinths, pedestals, vitrines, etc.—might be described as "sculptural." Mostly composed of stacks of MDF boards laser cut into curvilinear, undulating shapes, these otherwise reticent items of museological infrastructure here assume a heightened presence, suggesting both the sedimented topographies of archeological digs and a futuristic architecture.

JT Arles is of course a site with an important history in modern art. How does your work there relate to the precedents of Impressionist and Post-Impressionist painting, let's say?

JP Yeah, well, Van Gogh made something like four hundred paintings in that region.

JT So, this is a kind of painting that has all to do with optical mixing. Instead of mixing their colors on the canvas, these artists placed them side by side, and our impression of the painting's color is due to what happens between those little spots of paint. And maybe the floor you were talking about is now doing something like that?

JP I wanted there to be a referential condition to what I did there, but a very loose one. You have to do a lot of gymnastics with that floor to turn it back into an Impressionist painting—which is good. If it's something that happens, that could be construed as site-specific.

JT On that point, I was looking around the room I'm staying in [at Pardo's house in Mérida], and it occurred to me that in the design of the tilework or the cabinetry there is always an attempt to never fall into an ornamental rut, to always thwart symmetry and patterning. This is not to say that the design does not gel into one thing, a kind of all-over experience, but when you focus on the details, they always come apart.

JP Yeah, I like things that make time, where you have to look at them and process them. Because patterns, generally, are different; they're like sound-bites; they totalize. When you look at the floor

59 Pardo's incursion into the Musée des Augustins is confined to its Hall of Roman Sculpture, and is focused mainly on its extensive collection of twelfth-century Romanesque capitals. These have been replaced atop sleek tubular columns painted with colored bands that go from raw sienna to slate blue, and mimic the striated chromatic design of the partial walls erected all around the space. The outcome is an immersive yet acutely bipolar environment where elements of antiquity collide with elements of modernity, neither side subsuming the other. As a finishing touch, Pardo hung one of his signature lamps above every capital. "If you want people to spend a little more time with these things," he told me, "you stick a kind of Brazilian Mardi Gras hat on them." Here, as with the LACMA installation, museum didactics were downplayed in favor of aesthetic free play. The project was completed for the Toulouse International Art Festival in the summer 2014, and remains on view.

in the house, there's a limited amount of colors, there's a limited amount of shapes, but they have to be designed like a sort of painting. So, that's how they're worked out on the computer, and then they're transposed into the actual space.

JT So, what you're trying to do with this limited register is to obtain maximal difference?

JP Yeah, because I believe that that might be more interesting. It puts forward the notion of a picture versus a pattern, or a picture that initially is seen as a pattern. So, there's a kind of reversal that occurs...

JT ...Because pattern, décor, is allowed to recede; it's everywhere the same. But a picture comes forward in its singularity.

JP It's about making you want to look everywhere.

17

ART AND HOUSING PORTRAITURE SCALE

Mérida
September 2019

It seems that Jorge's work is never done, and this is because socializing is such a substantial part of it. During the five nights I stayed at his home, only one was not spent entertaining the seemingly nonstop stream of guests; this sole exception occurring only because we had been invited to dinner at someone else's home. We were constantly surrounded by people, which meant that my conversations with Jorge were often confined to a series of relatively brief interim periods. The one that follows again took place in the car, as we drove to and from the local Costco—another sign of how this area had transformed. No doubt, this big-box destination had exerted some influence on our talk, which mainly circles around questions of scale. If Jorge's work can generally be classified as sculpture, then scale is one of its most crucial elements, yet for him this does not simply come down to a matter of relative size—whether within the work, or between works, or between works and their contexts. There is also a scale to ideas, and then another scale to their accessibility, he suggests while asking, "Can you have a tiny audience for a really big idea?"

JT Your concern with housing begins with *4166 Sea View Lane*, and shortly thereafter you designed the private home in Puerto Rico for Cesar and Mimma Reyes, and then the dormitory in Skive, Denmark. *Tecoh* and *L'Arlatan* are the most grandiose realizations of your house-that-is-also-a-sculpture conceit. But, in between these projects, there are several works and exhibitions where you deal with housing on a more modest scale, and maybe also more abstractly.

JP Well, I built some houses for myself—here in Mérida, in Long Island, and in New York. And I also did these shows that enter the space of the exhibition as architecture, and I find these projects interesting because, at that point, I'm not making it happen anymore;

I'm not imposing that architectural frame on the object. It's more like drawing an imposition on that through the history of the other projects.

JT   A few of these shows have a houselike quality—for instance, the one you did in Miami with Bonnie Clearwater. (*Jorge Pardo: House*, December 4, 2007–March 2, 2008, Museum of Contemporary Art, North Miami) (fig. 21).

JP   Yeah, so there we took the interior of *4166 Sea View Lane* and just sort of mapped it onto the exhibition space, and that was more for scenographic reasons. We thought it would be interesting that the space would not be this white cube, but rather an abstraction of that house.

JT   Bearing in mind that the original house is also in a sense an abstraction inasmuch as it is also a sculpture, I wonder how exactly one should differentiate the abstraction that occurred in Miami. *4166 Sea View Lane* began as more of a sculpture than a house when it was open to the public and you had not yet moved in. But then, while you lived there, it became more a house than a sculpture. And finally when it was scenographically reconstituted in Miami, it was primarily as a sculptural experience. There is maybe again this movement of folding in and folding out at play here.

JP   I agree that that's sort of the purpose of doing those things. You want to get inside that optic you're describing to see what happens when you fold the work inside and out. Does the original sculpture become a prop? Or is it folded into a photographic project?

JT   You often talk about the ultimate destination of the artwork as a private one; no matter how site-specific it might be, it always winds up in—or, in your case, sometimes winds up *as*—somebody's home. The scenography in Miami, though, is paradoxically site-specific through and through. It takes account of the museum as a non-site, to go back to Smithson, but by relating it to a site, it is for a time specified. What you do there is set dressing, a kind of mise-en-scene, so it does not really transform what the museum fundamentally is, but it does make explicit the connection between public and private spaces of display. Site-specificity, for you, is something that is complicated: it is always public and private.

JP Yeah, one of the problems of how sited works are consumed is that their aspirations are not really very different from those of the white cube. Site-specificity always works to somehow limit the contextual origins of the work...

JT ...The origins *and* the destination of the work.

JP Exactly. So, I think that, instead of producing the possibility of a kind of agile misreading, it [site-specificity] wants to do exactly the opposite. Like the white cube, it wants to manage all the stuff that's unwieldy about art. And I like to think about place and location as something that, involuntarily, is always moving. One has to get trapped in a particular reading of the moment, and that's complicated to me because that's no longer about ideological discourse. If you think about why people came up with a notion like site-specificity, it's completely tethered as a polemic to something not being in the fucking gallery, right? That is the whole purpose of that term. You know, how do you still sustain the artfulness of the gesture in the thing, the object, or the place, without relying on the civility of the gallery? I think there's a conservative impulse in that, which I'm trying to optimally derange. I want to show a kind of irreverence toward the specificity of those terms, to show that they're much more unstable. I want people to lose all those certainties, to get lost in the work.

JT When people think about the private home as a destination for art, it is also as a kind of nonsite, a non-specific place, but it isn't really, is it? You often treat the home as a site.

JP Well, a private home, when it's described as a site, has to inscribe itself as a condition with problems that may or may not reinforce the artwork, and that's compelling to me because there's an inherent instability there.

JT So, getting back to your show in Miami, which becomes scenographically sited in your own home, this is where you also presented your bookshelf "portrait" of George Porcari (*Portrait of George Porcari*, 1995).[60] (fig. 22) So, there are other homes, other sites, that also appear there.

JP This is a piece that was originally shown at Tom Solomon's space, and then later at Petzel. And, in the end, all those books were all destroyed in Hurricane Sandy—it's kind of sad.

JT How do you make up for that?

JP You can't. You know, that book collection at Art Center that George put together over thirty years is important. When he recently retired, they hired some hotshot to replace him, but George is a book person, he *reads*. There were very few volumes in the library in the eighties when we started at Art Center, and he put together this collection that was very smart. So, this new guy came in and said, "You might want to change the collection," but they wouldn't let him do this until they made a study of what the value of the existing collection was. They did this study and realized that the only other library that has anything close to what George put together is the Getty, and after that they actually decided to make more space for it. George is an interesting guy, you know, he's nutty in the best way. He was constantly buying books for himself, but then he was also constantly throwing books away because he had this very limited space. George did crazy things: like when CDs came out, he decided that CDs were the future, and he traded in his very large record collection for around five hundred dollars' worth of CDs...

JT ... Now zero dollars of CDs; you can't even give these things away.

JP Right, and he probably had fifty or a hundred thousand dollars of vinyl (*laughs*). George was always decommissioning his own collection. But what I liked about that was that his collection was not encyclopedic, which is normally how people think about collecting.

60 *Portrait of George Porcari*, 1995, is a work consisting of several rows of shelves filled with books and framed photographs. George Porcari is a longtime friend of the artist. The two met while enrolled in the undergraduate art program at the Art Center College of Design, and then both went on to work at the school's library. Porcari was largely responsible for book acquisitions and hence left a significant mark on the library's holdings. The somewhat irregular construction of the shelving units in the *Portrait* reflect the design of the shelves in Porcari's own home, and the books and photographs placed on them were all acquired from his own collection.

JT So, this piece of yours not only commemorates your friendship, but performs a kind of service to your friend. The artwork in the gallery serves to free up more space in his home.

JP Yeah, right, so he got some money for those books and bought new books.

JT This is all very specific information, and so now I'm wondering, how small can an audience be for a work of art? This question comes back to your *Portrait of George Porcari*, because that's an exercise in that kind of thinking, isn't it?

JP Yes, exactly.

JT A little while back you mentioned this as a question of scale, and somewhere else in our conversation I recall you talking about "expansiveness."

JP So, yes, I like to talk about scale as a matter of expansion or contraction, and not necessarily as a matter of size. Maybe scale should be thought about as a dynamic rather than something, you know, fixed.

JT Yeah, that's a very compelling line of thought because essentially, we're talking about sculpture, which always has a literal scale.

JP So, what is the scale that the work needs to be in order to have a relation to the audience? How can one make it *reverberate*? Where does the problem of scale start and where does it stop? Can you have a tiny audience for a really big idea? And how does this manifest itself? I'm always thinking about stuff like that.

JT And this might also have to do with accessibility, because accessibility is maybe also a *quality* of the artwork. I mean, it's not necessarily a good or a bad quality; it's just an aspect of the work, an ingredient that an artist can play with. So, in regard to the *Portrait*, you could say that this work would be most accessible to the people that actually know George Porcari. And then, at the next level down, there's the people that recognize that this person after whom you've named your work is probably your friend: it's a friend of the artist's and he's made a kind of portrait of him. There's a tradition of artists making portraits of friends that you don't know, these anonymous people.

JP   Yes, there's this whole history of portraits that artists make of people that they've shared a life with. I made this other work in that vein; it was shown at the Guggenheim when they had a space on Broadway. (*Rooms with a View: Environments for Video*, April 16–June 15, 1997) (fig. 23) This was a two-person show with Tobias Rehberger, and they wanted to show video works, so he made these little TVs that hang like balls from the ceiling and I made these folding screens, you know, like what you might find in a lady's boudoir. I titled the work *Vince Robbins* after this very narcissistic teacher I had at Art Center. And I remember thinking, "OK, this guy is obsessed with being famous and is a question-able artist," and I was really curious about what would happen if I centralized him. I was really curious what he would *do* (*laughs*).

JT   Alright, so that's your motivation…

JP   But that could be rolled back to this question of the work's output in relation to scale, right? Because, at the end of the day, I was more interested in its particular impact on this person versus what it might do more generally in the gallery. So, I was thinking of how to marshal all the forces, the scale of this project—you know, it's at the Guggenheim—toward something much, much smaller.

JT   Again, that's your particular stake in the project, but what does this do for the general audience?

JP   But I was thinking of Vince Robbins as an audience, just an audi-ence of one.

JT   That's also what was interesting about your old friend Bob Weber: he also conceived of his works as having an audience of one. But that's a different situation in regard to, let's say, the psycho-logical dynamics at work here. I remember the show you did with Weber in Chinatown, and there your relation to this person was laid out in the press release.[61] Here, though, the name Vince Robbins is left dangling. You wonder if this person is being cele-brated or ridiculed.

JP I like that space because it is unstable. You have to input the data of whatever you collect in your head into the work. Years later, he sent me an email asking, "Why did you use my name?" And I never wrote him back because I thought that would be much more annoying (*laughs*).

JT Well, besides the people that know of your relation to him, there might be those who say, "Oh, the artist gave his work a proper name—that's interesting." I mean, artworks aren't supposed to get proper names; they aren't people. That's maybe the lowest level of access...

JP ...It's got a lot of tributaries where you can go with it. And I was not unaware of those tributaries; it's just that there was this one tributary that I was most interested in because it was small. And, at the time, I was thinking along those lines with the MOCA house [*4166 Sea View Lane*] as well, because that also had to do with questions of scale. Because the show they proposed to me was in a diminutive space, and so I wanted to make something that would not fit in there. I was already thinking that it was funny and strange that the scale of sculpture is so concretized. Is there a way to deploy ideas of scale that is more dynamic in terms of thinking the work?

JT It's interesting that, today, a lot of artists talk about their involvement in shows, the space they are given on the wall, let's say, in terms of "real estate." That term, which we would never have used when we were in art school, is now common, right? But in the case of your house for MOCA, the idea is literalized: you were given a

---

61 In 1999, Pardo mounted an exhibition at China Art Objects featuring his own works alongside those of his former Art Center classmate and close friend Bob Weber, who had passed away in 1994. Weber was represented by several pieces of furniture, mostly seats that had been custom-built for their owners, reflecting their physical characteristics as well as their tastes and inclinations. Pardo's contribution was a series of glass lamps hung very high from the gallery's tall ceiling. I wrote a review of the show in which I mentioned "the elegiac nature of the proceedings," then adding this: "One could go on about how this served to throw the fetish-character of Pardo's objects into even sharper relief, but what really stood out was the supreme humility of the gesture by which he ceded way to the work of a lesser-known friend and allowed it, literally, to shine." ("Jorge Pardo and Bob Weber at China Art Objects," *Frieze* 48 [September/October 1999]: 103.)

smaller space and then made a bigger space—that's literally more real estate.

JP I didn't want more real estate, because, for me, the house was a Focus show. It's not about wanting something bigger; it's about wanting to see what happens when something big gets stuck in something small; it's very different. I wanted to think about the *trauma* of something like that.

JT So you produce this convulsion, maybe, between the expansive and diminutive perspective. And, as a viewer, one also understands that this work, which is on view for just a short time, will then not be on view, while still remaining in place. So, there also the view narrows to an audience of one—that is, to you as the person who lives in the house. I've always found that fascinating as an idea, because, strangely, it's an idea that has to be made public. The idea of the audience of one has to be shared somehow with the broad public.

JP Right. And also it wasn't about exposing any part of my life in the process. It's not like Andrea Zittel, who wants people to come out to the desert and see her living in a compound. I want to have a private life.

JT With *Tecoh*, the spooky aspect maybe has to do with the fact that here we're left thinking of an audience of *none*.

JP (*Laughing*) Better yet than the audience of one is the audience of none!

JT I mean, certainly we were there, but we could imagine no one being there. And here also the notion of scale is thrown into sharp relief, because the space is so opulent, the architecture so big, and the more expansive the ground, the more that has been done there…

JP … The more that notion of audience sort of compresses and intensifies.

Fig. 21a *House*, 2007. Installation view, Museum of Contemporary Art, North Miami.

Fig. 21b *House*, 2007. Installation view, Museum of Contemporary Art, North Miami.

Fig. 22 *Portrait of George Porcari*, 1995. Installation view, Thomas Solomon's Garage, Los Angeles.

Fig. 23 *Vince Robbins*, 1997. Installation view, Guggenheim Museum Soho, New York.

18

THE HACIENDA GARDENS PHENOMENOLOGY HYSTERIA

Mérida
September 2019

Jorge's house in Mérida is comprised of three stand-alone buildings that sit in a row. These are rendered invisible to the street by a high wall, which opens onto a garage, which in turn opens onto a space that serves as a living room and dining room. Next is a building boasting a large open kitchen, a dining table, and some more casual furnishings congenial to after-meal conversation. Finally, in back, is a two-story structure with three bedrooms on each floor. Between these three buildings are two gardens lushly planted with a host of outsize native specimens, mini-jungles. This relatively short conversation deals with landscaping, which, beginning with *4166 Sea View Lane*, has become an integral element of the artist's house-that-is-also-a-sculpture scheme.

JT Gardens aren't really shown in Mexico; they are hidden behind the walls of the hacienda.

JP The hacienda is really a Spanish or Moorish design, where there's these street-facing walls and doors you go through, but inside there's gardens, there's water, there's all these things that don't exist so readily in these regions. So that typology was used here a lot. You have these streets that are, like, seventy inches wide, but when you go inside, there's a huge amount of property. It's Moorish; you know, Arabs ran Spain for around three hundred years.

JT There is this dichotomy between a very prosaic front and the opulent, even Edenic, space in back.

JP Yeah, there's no impulse to share your front yard.

JT This "sharing of the front yard," as you put it, is a very American concept, isn't it? Maybe "sharing" is not the right word for what is going on with the up-front display.

JP I haven't really researched it, but historically I think that people only started growing grass lawns once they had made enough money not to have to use their land for farming. That's why all those grand Southern plantations had big lawns; it was a way to show their wealth. And from that comes the American front lawn; it's like a petit bourgeois impulse toward grandeur, and maybe we can mix in some sort of puritanical paranoia over money (*laughs*).

JT   What you're saying with your lawn is, "This is where we come from; we started as farmers." But then you are also saying, "This is where we now are; we are no longer farmers." Once the land is used for these decorative purposes, it takes on a purely symbolic value. Also, a lot is made of the fact that the front lawns in American suburbs connect all the way up the street. They become symbolic of what connects us, but, as you say, it's also a space of paranoia.

JP   I've always found front lawns to be the most depressing things about American architecture. They take up about thirty percent of your land, and they're usually dead. They only get used on the Fourth of July. But if you could build a tall wall in front of it, then you could actually use it like an outdoor room.

JT   So, everywhere, people in Los Angeles are tearing up their front lawns and replacing them with drought-tolerant plantings. Or else they are actually trying to grow something edible there—a return to the farming thing that's somewhat chic. So, grass is seen as wasteful, you know, from the ecological perspective, but it's also seen as passé, uncool.

JP   The front lawn is technically a way to green up the streets. That's the best side of it, but there are obviously other ways to accomplish this.

JT   You know, there is a downside to what's going on now, with everyone expressing their political positions and their moral values and their tastes through their front yards. They are all so differentiated, or there's a very competitive effort to make them so. When the grass lawn was the status quo, it was maybe easier to fit in.

JP   Basically, just get rid of that shit, and put a wall up (*laughs*).

JT   OK, in this regard, I was going to ask you what you think about Robert Irwin's garden for LACMA (*Primal Palm Garden*, 2010).[62]

This was produced at a time when the front lawn had already earned its bad reputation in California. Anyone left with a front lawn was quickly becoming associated with such things as golf courses and Republicanism, a very nostalgic sort of value system. So, Irwin went "whole hog" with this—it's a whole lot of lawn—which struck me as a controversial move when you consider the ostensibly liberal context.

JP   But you need a lot of lawn in public spaces. His shtick is more about putting in these very esoteric palms.

JT   Even the palms seem nostalgic. No one is planting palms in L.A.; palms are being torn down.

JP   I don't understand his gardens, to be honest. They're all very structured. You don't really get a lot of bang for your buck. Except maybe for that one at the Getty, which is much more opulent.

JT   But what's interesting to me about the LACMA garden is that it almost seems to be *about* Americana. I sense a kind of ambivalence in this design that is compelling.

JP   That garden seems lost there...

JT   Sometimes it happens that artists, at a late stage in their careers, produce a kind of work that seems utterly characteristic, predictable to a point of banality—it's just the brand showing itself again—but in a more covert way, maybe, they might actually be dealing with something quite loaded. This can appear within those works that are the most outwardly anodyne. That's how I was thinking of Robert Irwin's garden for LACMA. To begin with, the amount of surface area

62   Robert Irwin's garden for LACMA (on which he collaborated with the land-scape architect Paul Comstock) was largely developed around the motif of the palm tree. Over a hundred palms were dispersed throughout the museum campus, with an emphasis on "primal" varieties, as per the work's title—a nod to the nearby La Brea Tar Pits, with their dinosaur displays. Included alongside the palms are several species of cycads and tree ferns, all growing out of green lawn beds. Irwin's design is partly a pushback to Los Angeles City Council decision to scale back on the planting of palms in favor of native trees, "which I thought was an odd idea," he is quoted as saying by The Horticult, "because they're almost a symbol for the city. I suggested, 'No, let's do the opposite.'" See: https://thehorticult.com/best-fronds-inside-robert-irwins-primal-palm-garden-at-lacma/. Accessed August 22, 2020.

that is given over to a green lawn should strike everyone in Los Angeles today as egregious. There's a kind of covert aggressiveness about Irwin's decisions, even though they come off as placid and meaningless.

JP He's a good artist. I personally don't understand those strategies—they seem to belong to my parents—but I'm very respectful of them. That's almost a generational notion from when artists believed that there were certain effects that could be achieved by managing geometry properly, or something like that.

JT OK, but what I was thinking about had less to do with any of the standard readings of phenomenology ...

JP ... I don't think that he cares about any of the stuff you're talking about ...

JT ... He doesn't have to care about it. I'm just saying that it might be rearing up in his work in some way.

JP Yeah, what you're describing is there; it's just that it is highly sublimated.

JT What would the work of a grumpy phenomenologist be? You know, when you can't maintain the Zen attitude in your everyday life, and some of your irritation starts to show up in the work?

JP It's complicated because anyone who is involved in a phenomenological pursuit has to occupy a space of hysteria to some degree. So I would say the grumpy phenomenologist is actually someone like Pae White, who really wants these sorts of funny excesses of form to take you out of yourself, to reach a pitch that you either love or have to run from. People who are obsessed with phenomenology, they find shiny shit and can't stop looking. And there's a sense that your faculties for observation and processing are somehow being deadened by this thing. There's a minimum amount of hysteria required for that kind of pursuit.

JT Your faculties are deadened or refreshed by this experience?

JP They're being arrested. Language is being arrested through an intense and unmanageable opticality. There are so many colors that it stops you in your tracks. Pae White is maybe the best at it, and that's because Pae actually comes from someone like Irwin. She bought Light and Space, the whole kit and caboodle. I'm not being negative; that's just the way it is…

JT I think that, at one time, when I was at school, Irwin, and in particular his lectures, were pretty revelatory. There's a very welcome aspect to what he says about the denial of the ego, or getting past it—again, that Zen aspect.

JP There's always an aspect of suspension, a suspension of disbelief, but then if the work employs enough hysteria you can forget that you're suspending disbelief.

JT Hysteria is such a cosmopolitan Western word, isn't it? I think that hysteria exists, but it's on the opposite end of Zen.

JP I don't know if hysteria exists; it's a problematic term stemming from the Greek word for uterus.

JT There is such a thing as male hysteria. This is a complete side note, but I came across a description in a sociology or ethnography text of some Indigenous tribe where the men undergo the whole birthing process along with their women. They fantastically give birth right beside them; that's a kind of pronounced hysteria. Hysteria is innate in both men and women, I'd say.

JP I don't think it's innate. It's the product of stimuli. And sometimes there is a kind of metaphoric operation in it, and sometimes there's myth running through it. If you look deep enough you can always find this whole host of language triggers that it responds to.

JT Put simply, it's a very elaborate form of acting out.

JP It works.

JT Psychological problems, irresolvable conflicts, are acted out in very elaborate patterns…

JP   ... In all sorts of crazy ways. Yes, basically that is what we've been talking about. It is a behavior, but do these people *have* hysteria? I don't know. Freud mined it to such a degree that it lost its gender (*laughs*). But really there has to be a way to talk about this stuff. We started with phenomenology ...

JT   ... Yes, and then you brought hysteria into it, and that's interesting because you're suggesting that while you are having this transformative experience ...

JP   You're experiencing the sublime, basically ...

JT   ... And you're ostensibly leaving yourself, but all the while, you're acting out, and you're doing so neurotically, hysterically.

JP   That always made the most sense to me. And, you know, in the future, there will be pills for this (*laughs*). Pills that do both: pills that produce the condition and pills that help manage it.

19

LANGUAGE

THE ABSTRACT AND THE CONCRETE

OVER-CODING

COMPLEXITY

Mérida
September 2019

How does one bring what started out as an endless conversation to a conclusion that is at least provisionally satisfying? I did so by breaking the editorial rule I had set for this project of sticking to chronological sequence. This particular encounter occurred earlier on in my trip, but is presented at the end because it entailed some reflection on just what it was that we had been doing together throughout the years. I try again to get Jorge to define his aesthetic, which could be seen to refer to aestheticism as such, while at the same time indexing every formal move to a complex order of social circumstances. I try to get him to put these operations into words, but mostly we speak about the words themselves.

JT   I've been thinking about these words that pass between us, and about what purpose they serve or don't serve. I mentioned sometime earlier—this was in 2012, after reading your interview with Alex Coles—that your thoughts hadn't changed so much over the years, but that, here and there, a new word creeps in, and this obviously has an effect on how one understands your practice. The new word that jumped out at me at that point was "fragility," which you used to describe your work to him. Fragility relates to the contingencies that you've discussed with me on many occasions—this notion of remaining open to the contingencies—but I'd say that it reframes that argument somewhat. Anyway, I looked through the entire transcript of our conversation and found that you did not use this word once in there—except for that time that I brought it up. Are you conscious of using different words when speaking to different people?

JP   Well, only in the most general way. I mean, you have different audiences that you engage with in terms of discussion, and with some of them you share more of the process of your formation than with others, and so the language changes in that way. Like, for instance, when I speak to students, that'll be a different vocabulary than I would use with you. So, of course, there is always a kind of presupposition being made about the recipient, but I'd say that it's not so much about reading *them* as responding to the conditions of the day in which we are speaking. The word "fragility" sounded good in relation to what Alex and I were talking about. Normally I'd use another word, but "fragility" worked best there to describe how easily the work can be misread.

JT   In a way, it's a more passive term than some of the ones you've used with me—terms like "corruption" and "contamination," for instance. These are quite aggressive.

JP   So, what Alex was trying to get at is that artists should construct a discourse for what they do in the studio, and it has to be very particular. Some artists even hire writers and PR people for this purpose, but I've never done that. I'm much more interested in having conversations that reflect the operations of thinking rather than *projecting*, let's say, ideologically and discursively. There's very little interesting writing about my work—I mean, I don't write about my work—but there are a lot of interesting interviews. And that's OK. I think that that's what I was trying to say with "fragility," because Alex really saw that as a lack in the work, like a missing bulwark or something, and my thinking is that fragility is OK.

JT   So the word arises in the course of your ongoing discussion with this person; it's the product of "the conditions of the day," as you said, and these conditions are interpersonal, and they evolve over time.

JP   You know, I don't think it's very productive for critics to "get" artists. You should, in my book, be able to swap your discourse around. Because what we're talking about could be fodder for something else, six months or ten years from now. It could be productive on both ends. I'd rather stay away from any endgame.

JT   That's good, but there have been a few moments between us when I can sense that you are becoming impatient, and it's almost like you then try to school me.

JP   Generally, what you might sense as impatience is probably just me disagreeing with something you've said.

JT   Right, absolutely, and then you assume a tone that's almost that of a teacher.

JP   And then I try to bring it back around. I think, "What am I thinking? Let me think about this a different way, because I don't like how the work is being read, but maybe I can find some middle ground where we'll both be happy." You know, that's what's going on in my head (laughs).

JT   Generally, these moments of disagreement are ones where I display what could be construed as a kind of Romanticism.

JP   Generally, it's when you bring in these sorts of historical landing points, whereas someone like me is more used to just walking through them.

JT   So, again, I've been rereading the transcripts of all our conversations, and what really struck me on the last pass is that there is a kind of dichotomy in your thinking, or again, in your language. For all your insistence on materiality and baseness, there is also an overwhelming tendency to get abstract—and I'm not sure if that's exactly the right word here. But whenever you bring up something that's real and grounded, it always turns quickly into an idea, something that exists only in the mind.

JP   Yeah, the discussion of these objects, these materials, and these processes, all of that anchors you so that you can start to sort of *reverberate* through abstraction as a means of description, or as a way to account for the phenomenon. If we weren't doing that, we'd be compiling an index; this is different. We're dealing with *interpretation* here, a reading. That's why it might seem like we're disassociating from the object when, in the end, we're not. The object has to be grounded in the particulars of how it's made, what it's made of, how it's shown, how many times it's been shown, what other things have been shown that are related to it, etc., but then very quickly it becomes about a set of relationships that are more complicated.

JT   A word like "speculative," for instance, is a very abstract word.

JP   Sure, and, at the end of the day, that word can be brought back to a very simple wish to analyze. Because you have to imagine what this thing is going to *do*—you know, how is this object going to work, or how are these materials going to behave? I use the word "speculative" because I don't really feel that I can control those operations other than through language. So, that's probably why the discussion becomes abstract really fast.

JT   This word "speculative" is like a tool: it opens a space in the object, and it allows you to meditate not just on it, but in a way, inside it.

JP   It's a tool that capitalizes on the object in a reverberatory way. I think that many people speak of objects abstractly without realizing that they are being abstract. Because 99.9 percent of the discourse, the writing, the hearsay, or whatever that's associated with the consumption of an art object happens in the head. It is entirely an abstraction.

JT   But when one says something like, "This color red makes me feel warm," would that be more or less abstract?

JP   That's very abstract, because it's dealing with a contingency; it's not landing on anything real. You know, feelings are abstract.

JT   In your own language you tend to connect feelings about things, or feelings derived from perception, to ideology. This, to me, makes the whole process of description even more abstract in a way.

JP   That's interesting. But that's maybe also just the drift of this discussion. We've been talking a lot about the Cold War, about commies versus capitalists, and so on.

JT   Right, so this opposition is what allows one to say things like, "This painting makes me feel free" versus "This painting makes me feel like I'm being co-opted by the state."

JP   I don't really *feel* works. I don't read them through feelings; that's not what I want from art. I'm someone who takes pleasure in being lost in a work, and that doesn't have anything to do with any kind of positivism.

JT   Well, even the desire to get lost in a work implies some sort of position, an ideology. Now, of course, when *you* say something like that, it's going to impact the way that people read your work. That's maybe one function of a book like this one we're working on. Your comments become prescriptive.

JP   But there's always the possibility that I could be completely wrong. So, when we do speak abstractly, we're trying to open up the possibilities for interpretation. I mean, when you make a work it's with the assumption that its most fundamental result is discourse in some sense, whatever flavor you want. When you're listening to me, you're getting a very particular read on contemporary ideas about aesthetics and politics—you know, what I think is progressive or regressive, which works are more open and which are more didactic, things like that. For me, the politics are always there.

JT   So, when I say ideology, it's with the assumption that ideology is in a way the ultimate abstraction. Marx, for instance, would equate ideology with false consciousness.

JP   But really, it's no more or less unreal than saying, "Red makes me feel warm." That's not data; that's a fucking interpretation. Blue could make you feel warm.

JT   Blue could make a certain person feel warm, yes, but then there's always more to it than the feeling. For instance, you might feel warmly toward the blue because it makes you think of heaven. Or you might feel warmly toward the red because it's Coca-Cola red, and you like this product. Or you like it because it symbolizes a certain kind of American freedom; I think that this is certainly the way my parents would have felt about it when they were locked down in Czechoslovakia.

JP   Right, the red then becomes a linguistic operation. If you start to whack away at it, you're going to realize that there's all these leaps and bounds that have to be made in order to have that ideology referenced through this color. And that becomes abstract in a bad way, you know? I'm not interested in symbology; I'm much more interested in metaphor, which is something that lends itself to abstraction much more readily, or less precisely, because it enters into the poetic. I like hearsay, for instance, and the kind of abstraction that comes from that.

JT What about the possibility that ideologies, for all their abstraction, sometimes do, in a real way, attach to forms?

JP They do not. They are read through forms and that's very different than to be attached to a form. Nothing ideological ever becomes attached to a form.

JT What about a historical attachment?

JP That's a reading. Maybe I'm overstating it, but this is related to the dichotomy that we started with. I'm always aware and I play up the fact that we are talking about inanimate objects. What's important about works of art is that they don't move; they're like rocks. One of the most troubling aspects of criticism is that there's often a kind of deep aspirational desire in having these objects speak to you directly, with no metaphor, you know? The sixties were all about that. Even an artist like Serra believes that your relationship to the mass, the weight, or the density of the thing you're standing in front of is somehow *speaking*—it is not. It is provoked to be read it that way. This is all abstraction, all ideology, and that's why it has to be taken apart.

JT These ideological attachments—no matter how spurious, historical, or, to use your word, "contingent" they might be—nevertheless gain traction in discourse. So, going back to the Cold War, Abstract Expressionism is contrasted with Socialist Realism, and this is what allows one to define an ideological stake in formal matters, or matters of style. For example, Pollock's gesture comes to stand for a kind of improvisatory freedom that could be related to jazz, let's say, but only because it is being seen in opposition to a more constrained sort of gesture on the other side.

JP But exactly in the way you just described this, it is clear that we're speaking in abstractions. There's nothing concretized in any of it. You can reach a kind of critical mass in the use of this language that makes us agree, and this turns the object into a kind of useable sign. It's more about expediency than abstraction when we rely on those things to plug an entity into an object. I don't believe that entities exist in things. I think that things exist as they are, and we read them, and we impose readings on them, and those impositions can become very general when they reach a critical mass ...

JT   ... That's the key term here: "critical mass."

JP   Yeah, and this critical mass is an abstraction.

JT   It's when an ideology becomes influential, when it actually begins to affect the object in front of you.

JP   But it's still only a part of discourse. A material can have critical mass. Like, a bomb can have critical mass when it explodes and kills you, and this is something it would do with or without your input. But there is no artwork without you, that's the point. That's why I have a job and why you have a job. Our job is to make these things dance.

JT   Right, our job is to fold and to unfold these objects, and this is a process without an end. For instance, now, in the West, we know that there was not only one kind of Socialist Realism; there were many different kinds, with a more or less Realist aspiration within them. Some maintained more of a connection to a prior avant-gardism—to Futurism, let's say. And on the other side, we can look at Pollock today and say that this painting was not really free at all; it adhered to a kind of training that was predetermined in all sorts of ways; it was constrained by all of these factors.

JP   Right, and if you want to look at the painting that came after Pollock, you need to think that way. You have to think of the limits on what has been produced, because if you treat the object as an entity that speaks directly to you, you're basically turning it into a relic. The way relics operate is basically through celebration; you need to throw parties for them. There's no such a thing as direct emission of ideology.

JT   Nevertheless I have to say that you do *enjoy* talking about ideology, even if it is recognized as a function of discourse in relation to something that can't really be known.

JP   Yeah, ideology is interesting to speak about and to try to take apart because its whacked out; it's one of the most abstract things in human history.

JT   And it makes people do things.

JP   It permeates their minds to the extent that they could kill you (*laughs*).

JT   I don't know if there was a time that was more ideological than the Cold War, this period we come from. You can definitely see with younger people today that they don't have the same stake in ideology, in ideological positioning, or in these sorts of reductive operations.

JP   I would say this differently. I would say that we lived in a period where we were sold a bill of goods, and we were also given these tools to pick apart ideology, which could then be instrumentalized in whatever direction we wanted. I think that ideology is always functioning; there's no more or less of it today. But after the war, in what was maybe the most interesting time in art since the Renaissance— that is, the sixties—there were a lot of people who worked to set up almost a kind of schematics for ideological absolution. There was this assumption that, if you use these tools, you could be liberated from it. And I think that is why it appeared that there was so much ideology; it's because there were so many mechanisms that were put in place to help you pretend that you can manage that shit.

JT   Today, you manage ideology by buying a pair of Tod's shoes, for instance. This is the legacy of the sixties and the sort of instrumentalization of ideology that you speak of. What happens is that you can no longer produce a caricature of ideology because it has become so efficient.

JP   Sande Cohen always used to say that ideology is over-coding.[63] And over-coding is not a term that's used anymore because the process, or the condition, has become so naturalized, because the amount of code that it took to send people to the moon is less than what you have on your phone. The idea of over-coding emerged because of the fetish of the computer's ability to process information so fast, so it worked metaphorically for a time.

63 Sande Cohen is a historian who taught critical studies in the fine art departments of Art Center College of Design and California Institute for the Arts in the eighties, when both Pardo and I attended these respective institutions. He was famous for his critiques of the academic milieu within which he operated, as is obvious from the title of his 1993 book, *Academia and the Luster of Capital*.

JT   This comes back to what you've talked about on several occasions as managing complexity, because clearly what we've been doing over time is managing more and more complexity. And there comes a point where it's not that you can't manage it anymore, but you stop trying to...

JP   ...It's about what flavor you want to manage it with (*laughs*). And that brings it back to aesthetics, because what you're constructing is a sense or an interpretation of how that complexity really feels.

Acknowledgments

Jorge and Jan would like to express their gratitude
to all who made this project possible: Tim Neuger and
Burkhard Riemschneider, whose enthusiasm kept
hope afloat during the downturn of COVID-19; Shannon
Harvey and Adam Michaels for their belief in this
book and sensitive design, with Dani Grossman, of
its contents; Eugenia Bell for her invaluable editorial
suggestions; Anna Maria Gonzales Cueva for further
editorial assistance; Dylan Lustrin for assistance in all
matters; and finally, Alexis Johnson and Won Ju Lim for
serving as the first readers of these conversations.

Image Credits

All images courtesy Jorge Pardo Studio unless otherwise noted.

pp. 26, 69, 115, 201: private collection, Berlin; courtesy neugerriemschneider, Berlin

pp. 27, 71, 157: courtesy Friedrich Petzel Gallery, NY

p. 113: photo by N. Koening; courtesy neugerriemschneider, Berlin

p. 158: photo by James Franklin

pp. 159–60: photos by Jody Asano; courtesy the artist and neugerriemschneider, Berlin

p. 202: photo by Jens Ziehe; courtesy the artist and neugerriemschneider, Berlin

p. 203: photo by Pierre Collet

p. 204 (top): courtesy Museum Associates/LACMA; (bottom): photo by Nicolas Brasseur

Jorge Pardo and Jan Tumlir:
Conversations
is published by

Inventory Press LLC
2305 Hyperion Ave
Los Angeles, CA 90027
inventorypress.com
&
neugerriemschneider
Linienstrasse 155
10115 Berlin, Germany

Editor: Eugenia Bell
Design: IN-FO.CO (Adam Michaels, Dani Grossman)

Printed and bound in Belgium by Graphius

ISBN: 978-1-941753-38-5
LCCN: 2020952312

Distributed by
ARTBOOK | D.A.P.
75 Broad Street, Suite 630
New York, NY 10004
artbook.com